Freeing Speech

Freeing Speech

The Constitutional War over

National Security

John Denvir

NEW YORK UNIVERSITY PRESS

New York and London

To
MIRIAM ROKEACH
Mate, Muse, and Editor Extraordinaire

NEW YORK UNIVERSITY PRESS
New York and London
www.nyupress.org

Library of Congress Cataloging-in-Publication Data

Denvir, John, 1942–
Freeing speech : the constitutional war over national security /
John Denvir.
p. cm.
Includes bibliographical references and index.
ISBN-13: 978–0–8147–2014–1 (cl : alk. paper)
ISBN-10: 0–8147–2014–5 (cl : alk. paper)
1. War and emergency legislation—United States.
2. Freedom of speech—United States. I. Title.
KF6075.D46   2010
342.73'062—dc22   2009048936

New York University Press books are printed on acid-free paper,
and their binding materials are chosen for strength and durability.
We strive to use environmentally responsible suppliers and materials
to the greatest extent possible in publishing our books.

Manufactured in the United States of America
10 9 8 7 6 5 4 3 2 1

Contents

Acknowledgments

I would like to thank my wife, Miriam Rokeach, for wholeheartedly supporting this project from the beginning and for making insightful comments on more drafts than either of us wishes to remember. Peter Honigsberg, Richard Delgado, Jean Stefancic, Jeffrey Brand, Charles Reich, David Fielding, David Rorick, Howard DeNike, Michael Denvir, Alex Tsesis, and Mark Tushnet also read earlier drafts and made helpful suggestions. I also would like to thank University of San Francisco Law School students Jason Fellner, LaRon Doty, Kevin Reilly, and Frank Kucera for their valuable research help and the staff at the USF Law library and USF Law Faculty Services for their excellent work.

Introduction

Constitutional Wars

The life of the law has not been logic;
it has been experience.

                         —Oliver Wendell Holmes

While I am not a great admirer of President George W. Bush, I must admit that he did much to energize public interest in constitutional law. Time and again after one of Bush's expansive uses of presidential power, students and friends would ask me, "Can he do that? Is it constitutional?" That turns out to be a question that will take a book to answer. The question itself assumes that the text of the Constitution draws bright lines between constitutional and unconstitutional actions. But the United States Constitution does not automatically churn out clear answers. It's a 200-year-old document whose authors employed broad language to govern a small former colony perched on the Atlantic coast and that offers few clear answers to the issues facing a twenty-first-century superpower. It is Supreme Court justices who give the text meaning relevant to today's issues. And the meanings they choose are fated to be controversial. To answer the question of the constitutionality of President Bush's uses of presidential power, we must reject the "one clear answer" picture of constitutional law and accept the fact that constitutional interpretation is an intellectual battlefield where different visions of our collective future compete for dominance.

Not only is certitude in short supply in constitutional argument; we must also accept that the competing constitutional visions are influenced by politics. In fact, they tend over time to reflect the political philosophies of the two major political parties. Liberal justices tend to favor expansive interpretation of congressional powers while conservatives resist such readings in order to support states' rights. With regard to individual rights, liberals argue for a broad interpretation of civil liberties like freedom of speech while most conservatives usually support the right of government to restrict such liberties. But when the issues involve individual rights affecting economic liberties, the positions are reversed; conservatives support robust interpretations that liberals oppose. All these opposing constitutional positions roughly mirror the respective ideological commitments of the Democratic and Republican parties. We should not be so surprised by this result since the justices themselves are selected by a political process.

I do not mean to suggest that Supreme Court doctrine evolves in lockstep fashion with the legislative programs of the major parties. Certainly individual justices have their own independent views that affect their votes. And the views of an individual justice evolve over time, sometimes away from the views of the party of the president who nominated him or her. The life tenure granted an individual justice also operates to provide more intellectual diversity since justices may stay faithful to policies that the party appointing them has abandoned. All these vagaries ensure that no one master vision ever becomes dominant across the broad array of constitutional issues. Instead, we find more localized wars over the proper interpretation of specific provisions of the constitutional text.

Four Constitutions

I think our discussions of constitutional issues such as Bush's use of his presidential powers will be more faithful to the complexity of this dynamic process if we keep in mind four different uses of the word "constitution": (1) the text, (2) the official Constitution, (3) the constitutional challenger, and (4) the de facto Constitution. The first refers to the actual written text. Here there is no controversy about the words used, but much controversy about what they meant originally and, more importantly, what they should mean today. The Constitution uses too many Delphic terms capable of too many intellectually acceptable interpretations to often give a clear answer to specific issues. It will help if we speak of the "official" Constitution. The official Constitution is the interpretation of the text chosen by the current Supreme Court majority. The official Constitution is what my students and friends meant when they asked whether Bush's actions were constitutional. But we can only know for sure the meaning of the official Constitution for actions that the Court has recently ruled upon because not only do the facts in every case differ but also there is always doubt about whether the current majority will stick with the official interpretation in a future case. Instead, they may choose an ideological rival to the official Constitution that I call the constitutional "challenger." The current official interpretation of presidential powers holds that the president must obey congressional laws in the area of national security, but conservative scholars support a rival position that rejects that interpretation. I hasten to add that the terms "official" and "challenger" do not represent a normative judgment about which interpretation is superior; they merely describe a political reality, a reality that is subject to change.

To make matters even more complicated, we should also note the "de facto" Constitution. This is the interpretation that actually operates when the Supreme Court has not spoken on an issue. It is especially important in the area of national security, where courts have often been reluctant to speak. For instance, even though the official Constitution says that the president must obey congressional laws, President Bush appeared to ignore a relevant congressional statute when he authorized the National Security Agency (NSA) to spy on American citizens in national security cases without obtaining a warrant. But the courts have refused to rule on the merits of cases challenging the legality of the NSA program on the technical ground that the plaintiffs did not have "standing" under Article III to bring the suit. This judicial silence means that the president's view of the extent of his powers, although at odds with the official Constitution, operated as the de facto constitutional rule in that dispute.

Here is a thumbnail sketch of the way I think constitutional interpretation actually operates. While citing the relevant section of the constitutional text is the opening gambit in most constitutional discussions, it seldom determines the outcome of a case. The actual process of making constitutional law consists of a competition between the official interpretation and its challenger. Most constitutional conflicts are about whether the official interpretation of a constitutional text will stand or whether it will be replaced by its rival. But the de facto Constitution is also important in the area of national security because of self-imposed limitations on what cases courts will hear. This cycle then repeats itself over time. Challengers become official and new challengers arise.

Accepting this dynamic model of constitutional interpretation has dramatic effects on the way we discuss constitutional issues. First, it explains why constitutional rulings are so controversial. Once we recognize that a justice's political vision does and should affect his or her decision, we can no longer be surprised that equally intelligent justices will come to different conclusions in any single case. Also, we will be suspicious of any advocate who attempts to end discussion by appealing to some single criterion (like "original intent") that claims to produce a single "right" answer to any issue. There will always be more than one intellectually respectable answer to any constitutional question. We should expect conflict and realize that it makes sense to listen carefully to our opponents' arguments, if only to better refute them.

And while this ideological war is waged over the proper result in every individual Supreme Court case where litigants attempt to secure the five-vote majority necessary to win, we should also recognize that the outcome of the larger war is determined by the appointment power of Article II that allows presidents to appoint Supreme Court justices subject to Senate approval. Over time the political visions of the justices determine the content of the official Constitution more than the briefs they read. Citizens have little impact on the Court's individual decisions, but they can have a large role in determining who is appointed and confirmed as a justice. Therefore, constitutional argument must go beyond just briefs to the Court to include works that help educate citizens so they can better play their role in the selection of justices. My hope is that this book will do just that.

A Court of Higher Politics

Some readers may be alarmed by my frank acceptance of a political dimension to constitutional interpretation. I wish to make clear that I do not think that judges should be political in the same way as legislators are. The Supreme Court is not a third legislature. Legislators have few controls on their discretion other than the need to be reelected. Justices, on the other hand, do not have to worry about reelection but are limited by the demands of the judicial role. We expect judges to decide cases within a tradition of rational argument that ignores the short-term political calculations that legislators engage in every day. We would have no qualms about a legislator who admitted that his or her vote was influenced by party loyalty, but a similar admission by a judge would be a clear violation of his or her duties as a judge.[1] In this way, the Supreme Court operates as a court of higher politics, influenced by political ideals but immune from short-term political pressures.

A Supreme Court that acts as a court of higher politics provides some real benefits for democracy. The appointment of Supreme Court justices for life removes the individual justice from the passions of partisan political debate at the same time that the political nature of the appointment process ensures that the Supreme Court as an institution is democratically accountable. And when we see the Court make a decision that we believe is "wrong," we can take comfort in the fact that in the long run the Court's work is controlled by the democratic process. "Wrong" interpretations are subject to correction by the same democratic appointment process that created them. The clear message is that if you are unhappy with the Court's rulings, you should work to have justices with your political vision appointed. Presidential candidates should be questioned on their constitutional visions and Senate candidates should be pressed on whether they will vote against judicial nominees who support constitutional policies you oppose.

The National Security Presidency

We all remember the television images of President Bush deftly landing a jet fighter on the deck of an aircraft carrier in the Persian Gulf one morning in May of 2003 and then hopping out of his plane to stand in front of a conveniently placed "Mission Accomplished" banner to announce to a cheering audience of sailors the successful completion of military operations in Iraq. Some people probably still remember that morning as a source of national pride; others see it as evidence of imperial hubris. For me, the Bush "Mission Accomplished" stunt symbolizes the National Security Presidency. Our constitutional tradition prides itself on maintaining a system of "checks" and "balances" to prevent abuses of governmental power. But since the advent of the Cold War, there has been a movement to relax these checks and balances in order to grant the president extraordinary independent powers in the area of national security. Bush's landing on that aircraft carrier incarnated this "can do" vision of a president who as commander-in- chief will do whatever he deems necessary to protect American national security interests all over the globe.

Here was a president who could not only authorize combat operations but also personally carry them out. I question whether this militant vision of the presidency squares with our constitutional ideals or even makes us more secure.

The media spectacle created by the Bush landing also highlights another aspect of presidential power—the modern president's capacity to orchestrate elaborate media campaigns that employ sophisticated tools of mass persuasion to mobilize public support for his national security policies. Bush's "Mission Accomplished" team produced a spectacle that used Hollywood techniques to craft a powerful appeal to the television audience's emotions. The unanswered (even unasked) question is whether such massive propaganda efforts corrupt the reasoned debate on national security issues necessary to democratic government.

Finally, there is the issue of freedom of speech. What the television images did not show us is as important as what they did. No images of dissent were allowed that day. We saw no banners protesting the president's decision to invade Iraq that would counter the visuals of unanimous support for the president's policies. And had a flotilla of protesters appeared on the scene that morning, we can be sure they would have been quickly escorted far out of camera range by military authorities on grounds of national security. Freedom of speech is not only a basic individual constitutional right; it is also an important part of our structure of checks and balances. We have to wonder how well our system of free expression is working when only one side of a debate is able to make itself heard.

Perhaps it would be helpful if I provided a short preview of my argument. Chapter 1 introduces the National Security Presidency. This conservative vision claims extraordinary powers for the president in the area of national security, not only the right of the president to act without congressional authorization but even the right to ignore congressional legislation and individual constitutional rights when he feels they impede his programs. The National Security Presidency has never been endorsed by the Supreme Court. It is still a constitutional challenger. In fact, the current majority has rejected its most extreme claim that the president can ignore limits imposed by Congress.[2] But the Supreme Court has not rejected another controversial presidential claim: authority to initiate combat without congressional authorization. And the refusal by lower courts to hear many cases has permitted the National Security Presidency to become the de facto Constitution over a large range of governmental activities.

Chapter 2 studies the threat to democratic government created by the power of presidential speech. While it is obvious that the president has a right to communicate his views on both domestic and foreign policy issues, the modern presidency goes well beyond merely making its views known. The "Mission Accomplished" production is just one example of a much larger and more long-standing practice of modern American presidents: using large amounts of government resources to craft extremely sophisticated media campaigns to mobilize support for their policies. Not only do these media blitzes appeal more to emotion than to reason, but many recent American presidents have even felt entitled to mislead the American people in order to attain their national security goals. The crucial constitutional question is not whether the president can speak, but whether Congress can and should use its authority to limit such propaganda efforts where they undermine democratic debate.

Chapter 3 traces the recent history of the First Amendment. The Warren Court dramatically expanded free speech protections to open up the political system to dissenting voices. Since then Republican presidents have appointed conservative justices who have quietly abandoned the Warren Court legacy to construct a new official First Amendment that tilts heavily toward government authority and against open, informed public debate. My primary thesis is that the adoption of a broad vision of presidential power in national security affairs coupled with this current weak official interpretation of the First Amendment dramatically transforms American democracy for the worse.

We could easily see the following scenario become reality. A presidential candidate does not discuss national security affairs during the campaign, but in fact has ambitious foreign policy objectives he keeps to himself. Once elected, the president uses a terrorist incident as an opportunity to propose military action against a foreign country not involved in the incident. In support of his new policy he mounts a massive public relations campaign to persuade the public and Congress that the proposed military action is necessary to defend our country against attack. His speeches concentrate on emotional issues like fear and national pride. Some of his statements are half-truths, others downright falsehoods. But his critics are unable to point out the inaccuracies because the true facts are classified as state secrets unavailable to the Congress, the press, and the public. When groups attempt to organize demonstrations to protest the war, authorities prohibit or severely limit the demonstrations on grounds of national security or fears for public safety. When demonstrations do occur, scuffles between police and demonstrators result in the jailing of demonstrators and more presidential speech connecting all protesters, no matter how peaceful, with the alleged protester violence. The clear implication is that dissent itself is unpatriotic. If the war is not successfully completed before the president stands for reelection, he mounts another massive public relations campaign arguing that victory is near and that national honor requires that we "stay the course." Most readers will recognize that this scenario is not pure fiction; it is a composite snapshot of our political history from Vietnam to Iraq.

The First Amendment's Role

The first three chapters present the problem; the second three present a solution. The primary problem is the president's ability to dominate debate on national security; the solution is a First Amendment that makes sure that opposition voices are heard. Chapters 4 and 5 present a new challenger to existing First Amendment doctrine, a vision that will reanimate political debate both by making more information available to inform public discussions of national security and by making sure that groups opposing government policies have a realistic opportunity to have their voices heard. Chapter 4 argues that too much information is kept secret under the present constitutional regime. We need a First Amendment that guarantees the press access to information in possession of the government that voters need in order to evaluate the government's performance. While there are some military and diplomatic secrets that must be kept confidential, these should be the exception, not the rule. Furthermore, independent judges rather than self-interested government officials should make the final decision on whether secrecy is warranted.

Chapter 5 examines the crucial role that citizens groups play in our democratic debate. It is these free speech activists who first nurture ideas that challenge government policies and then organize activities to bring the new ideas to a larger audience. The First Amendment must not only protect the autonomy of these activist organizations from government harassment but also ensure that these groups are given full access to the public forum to make their case to the American people.

An Engaged Supreme Court

Since 9/11, courts have adopted a passive stance toward national security issues, preferring to trust the president's judgment on issues involving national security. Chapter 6 argues that this passivity constitutes a failure of their duty to say what the law is. The Supreme Court in particular has a duty to state clearly the legislative and constitutional norms limiting presidential power and to stand ready to enforce them if the president ignores them. Conservatives argue that such judicial activism is "undemocratic," but once we accept the inevitable political dimension to any judicial act, we see that such judicial engagement actually supports democratic values. Conservatives argue that every court ruling for individual rights is a defeat for democracy because presidents and legislators are elected while judges are not. I challenge this assumption on two fronts. First, court-enforced First Amendment rights are a necessary precondition to the full and informed debate that democracy (including the election of presidents and legislators) requires. Secondly, judges themselves have strong, although indirect, democratic pedigrees.

The afterword connects the main arguments in this book to a larger constitutional vision. It argues that First Amendment rights are not enough to support the debate democracy demands. We need court support of a wide panoply of human rights in order to create an informed citizenry. Such human rights range from personal rights like privacy to social rights like a first-class education. In short. we need a human rights constitution.

The Time Is Now

We must resist the temptation to think that the dangers this book describes ended with the Bush presidency. It is true that President George W. Bush pushed the claims of presidential supremacy to the extreme, but history makes clear that Democratic presidents were the original architects of the National Security Presidency, and all presidents, no matter what their party, have claimed ever-increasing powers over national security. The election of Barack Obama may result in a more moderate exercise of the powers claimed, but not a rejection of the existence of those powers. This leaves them available to later presidents. And President Obama is no less an avid and talented practitioner than Bush of the rhetorical capabilities of his office in the national security area. With regard to the First Amendment, we should remember that a majority of the current Supreme Court presently supports the narrow official interpretation of the First Amendment, and that this majority will be difficult to dislodge. So the constitutional war this book describes over presidential power and free speech is not yet over. We need a new official constitution that limits presidential power and expands human rights. The time to fight is now.

The National
Security Presidency

Power tends to corrupt, and absolute power corrupts
absolutely.   —Lord Acton

In the introduction, I mentioned President Bush landing a fighter plane on an aircraft carrier to announce military victory in Iraq. For me this scene symbolizes a vision of the presidency that presents a serious challenge to the official constitutional interpretation of presidential powers in the area of national security. For reasons I will explain later in this chapter, it is also the de facto constitutional view over a large range of governmental programs. I call it the National Security Presidency. It argues for the necessity of quick, decisive action to protect America from foreign enemies. Readers who have followed the newspaper headlines since 9/11/01 have a good idea of its basic outline. It claims that, as commander-in-chief of the armed forces, the president has a special constitutional duty to protect American lives and interests. Sometimes he can act in concert with Congress, but often he must act on his own authority either because there is no time for congressional deliberation or because he is acting on the basis of information that he cannot share with Congress. Sometimes the president must even disregard congressional laws and individual constitutional rights when they interfere with his national security responsibilities. When evaluating this vision of the presidency we should remember that quick, decisive, secret actions often prove to be wrong-headed, and they never have the same democratic legitimacy as decisions that are vetted by a more inclusive political process.

The Text

Whatever the merits of the National Security Presidency, it certainly was not the structure that the authors of the Constitution intended for the office of president. Even a cursory glance at the text of the United States Constitution (I set out the relevant provisions in the appendix) indicates that its authors intended Congress to be the senior branch of the national government. Not only are the powers of Congress given pride of place in Article I, but the text of that article dwarfs in size the provisions relating to the president in Article II and to the Judiciary in Article III. Even when we focus on provisions with "national security" relevance, the powers of Congress dominate. Congress has the power not only to declare war but also to punish "piracies and felonies committed on the high seas," "raise and support armies," "provide and maintain a navy," and "provide for organizing , arming , and disciplining, the militia." All these congressional powers are then expanded by the added grant to Congress of the power to "make all laws which shall be necessary and proper for carrying into execution" the other powers granted to any department of the national government.

In comparison, the powers of the president in the area of foreign affairs are both narrow and supportive. He is the "commander in chief of the army and navy of the United States and the militia," but this meant he was to manage the wars Congress declared. It was understood that the president also could act to repel a sudden enemy attack before Congress had time to meet and act, and Article II authorized him to "make treaties, provided two thirds of the Senators present concur." He also had the power to appoint cabinet officers like the secretary of state, subject to Senate confirmation. One presidential power, to "receive ambassadors and other public ministers," sounded mostly ceremonial in nature, but it would grow in importance as the office of the presidency evolved. And finally, the president is given the power (and the duty) to "take care that the laws be faithfully executed," that is, to administer the laws that Congress passes.

The National Security Presidency sees no substantive role for the Supreme Court to rein in its authority, but the text itself takes a different view. Article III gives the Court specific authority in cases with foreign affairs ramifications. Article III grants the Court jurisdiction over "all cases affecting ambassadors," "all cases of admiralty jurisdiction," and "controversies" between a "state, or the citizens thereof, and foreign states, citizens, or subjects."

Of course, it would be naïve to expect that the institutional design created to govern a small former colony in the eighteenth century would adequately serve the needs of a growing nation. Constitutions must evolve with the history of the nation they are intended to guide, and often the constitutional text lags behind the new reality. The ideal way for these changes to take place is by means of the formal amendment process of Article V, but the process of Article V is so complicated that it has seldom been used for major constitutional changes.[1] Instead, we have used the informal process of judicial amendment. The text remains the same, but the Supreme Court's reading of it changes. For instance, as the economy became more national in scope, the power of the Congress to regulate interstate commerce waxed as that of the individual states waned. But this important constitutional change did not take place by means of a formal amendment of Congress's power over interstate commerce in Article I; instead, the Supreme Court gave a more expansive reading to the old language.[2]

At other times evolution takes place by consensus; everybody agrees that a larger meaning should be read into the text. There can be no court case if no one disagrees. Article II grants to the president the authority to "receive ambassadors." Although it sounds like only a ceremonial power, this power (combined with his authority over the federal bureaucracy) came to be seen as a grant to the president of the power to direct foreign policy short of war, subject to congressional opposition.

And sometimes presidents have gone beyond the powers granted them in the text. For instance, sometimes presidents have ordered the use of force without congressional authorization, although the lion's share of these actions were (to quote conservative scholar John Yoo) "small actions to protect American property, citizens or honor abroad that had little risk of significant combat."[3] And usually there was tacit congressional approval for these actions, if not explicit authorization. There are, however, two historical examples in which a president has gone beyond this limited exercise of expanded power. The first involved Abraham Lincoln in the Civil War. After the South's firing on Fort Sumter, Lincoln took several actions without consulting Congress that appeared beyond the power granted him by the text. He raised armies, secured credit, suspended the writ of habeas corpus, and blockaded southern ports.[4] Lincoln claimed that all these acts were emergency powers granted him as commander-in-chief, even though the text refers to no such emergency powers. In his defense, Lincoln believed that the very life of the nation was at risk and that this emergency justified strong presidential action. Today few disagree with his decision. But we have to decide whether the same reasoning grants contemporary presidents similar powers today when they feel we are facing a national emergency. Most constitutional commentators do not think that the Civil War experience justifies the powers claimed by President Bush. We should remember that Lincoln was dealing with a problem—a civil war—that the text does not anticipate; the Constitution is silent on that issue. But President Bush was dealing with the problem of authorizing force against a foreign foe, a power that the text reserves to the Congress. So, too, Lincoln always made his actions public and asked Congress to ratify them while many of Bush's most constitutionally controversial actions were hidden from Congress and the public.

Franklin Roosevelt also stretched the limits of presidential power in World War II. Roosevelt did not initiate combat on his own; World War II was the last war declared by Congress. But prior to Pearl Harbor he did enter into an executive agreement that enlisted American military might on the side of Great Britain against Nazi Germany in apparent defiance of congressional neutrality legislation. Pursuant to the agreement, we gave the British fifty destroyers in return for the use of British military bases in the Western hemisphere. The destroyers were intended to be used by the British in the war effort against Nazi Germany. Despite the apparent conflict with congressional law, Roosevelt signed the agreement on the basis of a legal opinion from his attorney general, Robert Jackson. Jackson argued that the president's acts indeed were authorized by Congress. Critics both then and later have agreed that Jackson's opinion disingenuously provided a legal mask for illegal presidential action.[5] But Roosevelt's allegedly improper actions were quite modest compared with the claims of President Bush.

The Official Constitution

The current official Constitution of independent presidential power is found in the 1952 Supreme Court case of *Youngstown Sheet & Tube Co. v. Sawyer.*[6] The case involved President Truman's seizure of privately owned steel mills to prevent a strike that he believed would hinder the American war effort in Korea. The steel companies resisted on the ground that the president had no authority to take such an action without congressional authorization. The court majority, in an opinion by Justice Black, ruled against the president because he only had the power to execute laws that

Congress had passed and here Congress had not only not passed a law that authorized him to seize private property to avoid a strike but in fact had refused him that power. The president's power to execute the law meant only the power to follow the rule prescribed by Congress; here Truman was ignoring a congressional law. The Black opinion also ruled that the president's power as commander-in-chief of the armed services did not come into play since that power was limited to acts in a limited theater of war, not decisions affecting the whole economy. Therefore, Black categorically rejected Truman's claim.

Usually the majority opinion in an important case constitutes the official Constitution, but sometimes later courts prefer to rely on a concurring opinion instead. That's what has happened with regard to the *Youngstown* decision; later courts and scholars have passed over Black's blunt rejection of autonomous presidential power on the grounds that it was too mechanistic. Instead, commentators[7] and the Supreme Court itself have been more drawn to the concurring opinion in *Youngstown* of Justice Jackson. This was the same Robert Jackson who as attorney general had approved President Roosevelt's expansive use of presidential powers during World War II. Jackson, like Black, held Truman's act unconstitutional, but he saw the relationship between congressional and presidential power in more fluid terms. Jackson saw three situations with different constitutional ramifications. First, when the president acts with congressional authorization, his powers are at their zenith. And when he acts in opposition to the declared will of Congress, his powers are at their nadir. But Jackson posited a third possibility:

> When the President acts in absence of either a congressional grant or denial of authority, he can only rely on his own independent powers, but there is a zone of twilight in which he and Congress may have concurrent authority, or in which its distribution is uncertain. In this area, any actual test of power is likely to depend on the imperatives of events and contemporary imponderables rather than on abstract theories of law.

Perhaps because of its admired fluidity, Jackson's "twilight zone" created an area of constitutional ambiguity that has allowed presidents to quietly expand their power. I will argue in chapter 6 that we would be better advised to return to Justice Black's clear rejection of independent presidential power.

And, as the *Youngstown* decision itself illustrates in striking down Truman's action, both Black and Jackson agreed that the Judiciary constituted a third partner in the constitutional scheme of separation of powers. When there is a dispute about the relative powers of the two political branches, it is up to the judicial branch to determine what the Constitution requires. Jackson joined Black in ruling that Truman's actions were in defiance of the clearly expressed will of Congress and, therefore, were unconstitutional.

The Imperial Presidency

But while both the Black and the Jackson opinions in *Youngstown* were speaking of presidential power in terms of constitutional checks and balances, American presidents from Truman on were beginning to operate according to a different model altogether. Historian Arthur Schlesinger Jr. uses the term "imperial presidency" to describe a vision of presidential power over foreign affairs practiced by all the presidents from the Truman through the Nixon administrations, an era when presidents routinely authorized offensive military operations without the consent, or even knowledge, of Congress or the people. The Imperial Presidency is the institutional forerunner of George W. Bush's National Security Presidency.

One of Harry Truman's major contributions to the Imperial Presidency was his decision to commit the United States to a large-scale land war in Korea without congressional authorization. Truman claimed that Congress's ratification of the United Nations Treaty committed the United States to United Nations' missions like that in Korea, but a general treaty obligation can never substitute for the constitutional requirement that Congress declare a specific war. Truman's essential constitutional claim was that as president and commander-in-chief, the president has inherent authority to commit American troops to battle without congressional authorization. This went well beyond what President Roosevelt had claimed. Congressional leaders protested, but were never able to secure a legislative majority to challenge Truman's action.[8] Since Korea, America presidents have claimed this independent power to send American troops to fight wherever, whenever, and in whatever numbers they believe necessary to achieve American foreign policy goals.

Truman's second contribution to the Imperial Presidency was the creation of the Central Intelligence Agency (CIA). The National Security Act of 1947 that created the CIA gave it two sorts of responsibilities. One was providing foreign intelligence to the president to help him chart American policy, but the act also gave the CIA an ambiguous authorization "to perform such other functions and duties related to intelligence affecting the national security as the National Security Council may from time to time direct."[9] There is still some doubt as to what Congress intended by this vague language. Truman himself intended the CIA to be an intelligence agency rather than a covert action agency, but presidents after Truman interpreted this language as authorizing the CIA to conduct "covert operations" against "unfriendly" foreign governments and political groups. These covert operations included propaganda and financing political parties that favored American interests, but they also sometimes included financing and directing paramilitary groups in attempts to overthrow foreign governments and assassinate foreign leaders.[10] While the intelligence-gathering component of the CIA might well fit easily with the president's powers to conduct foreign policy, many of these CIA operations were secret wars initiated without congressional knowledge or consent. Often the CIA did not even tell the president what they were up to.

Most readers will share my surprise at discovering that the supposedly moderate Republican Dwight D. Eisenhower expanded presidential national security powers substantially during his two terms. It was Eisenhower who put the CIA in the business of toppling foreign governments. Unwilling to bear the expense of conventional warfare, he found "covert actions" by the CIA to be a cheap way of fighting the Soviet Union during the Cold War. In his Pulitzer Prize–winning history of the CIA, Tim Weiner notes that during the Eisenhower administration, the CIA undertook 170 new major covert actions in forty-eight different countries, including political, psychological, and paramilitary warfare.[11] These included major efforts to overthrow elected governments in Iran, Guatemala, and Indonesia. The operations in Iran and Guatemala were successful, at least in the short term, but Weiner argues that the overwhelming majority of such operations were abject failures, resulting in the needless loss of lives and waste of taxpayer dollars. In that vein, we should remember that it was Eisenhower who authorized the planning for the CIA-directed invasion of Cuba that resulted in the Bay of Pigs fiasco that so embarrassed President John F. Kennedy at the beginning of his term.

Eisenhower also dramatically expanded the realm of secrecy in American government. Of course, American presidents had claimed the right to keep certain categories of information secret from the Congress and the people since the beginning of the republic, but traditionally the ambit of confidential information was construed narrowly to include only military and diplomatic matters and conversations between the president and his closest advisors. It was the Eisenhower administration that extended the area of secrecy to all information generated by the internal deliberative processes of government by creating the new doctrine of "executive privilege." Between 1955 and 1960, Eisenhower administration officials refused information to Congress forty-four times on the basis of a claim of executive privilege, more than in the entire first century of American government.[12]

And the Eisenhower years also demonstrate that secrecy breeds deceit. Once a fact is declared secret, officials feel entitled to lie to protect its confidentiality. When the secret finally becomes public, more lies are needed to protect the reputation of the purveyor of the first lie. This all-too-common plot played itself out in the Eisenhower administration in terms of secret flights that Eisenhower had personally approved over Soviet airspace by American U-2 spy planes. When one of the planes was shot down over Soviet territory and the pilot captured, the White House and the State Department told the American people that no such flights had ever been authorized until finally press accounts of the true facts required them to admit the falsehood.[13] We will see that false or misleading public statements by high-level officials, including the president, became a recurring motif in American foreign and national security policy.

John F. Kennedy also believed in a powerful national security presidency. While there were 170 covert CIA operations in the eight years of the Eisenhower administration, the Kennedy administration launched 163 in less than three years.[14] The most notorious of these was the Bay of Pigs fiasco mentioned above, in which the CIA attempted to land a small anti-Castro army on the shores of Cuba. There was no consultation with Congress about the secret attack. After the failure at the Bay of Pigs, the Kennedy brothers authorized the CIA to assassinate the Cuban leader Fidel Castro.[15] Some believe that the attempts to assassinate Castro led to Kennedy's own assassination. It was one more sign of the growing cult of secrecy that the CIA never mentioned the attempts to assassinate Castro when questioned by the Warren Commission investigating Kennedy's death.

Perhaps Kennedy's greatest foreign policy victory occurred when he faced down Nikita Khrushchev in 1962 about the presence of Soviet missiles in Cuba. Kennedy stopped Soviet ships headed for Cuba, an act of war under international law. Here too the president felt no need to consult Congress, much less ask its permission, before taking action. And once again, secrecy played a large role. We now know that the actual agreement with the Soviets was that they would remove the missiles and the United States, in turn, would soon thereafter remove missiles positioned in Turkey aimed at the Soviet Union.[16] Khrushchev agreed to keep the American promise secret in order to protect Kennedy's political image at home. But this secrecy served to reinforce the militarist myth that confrontation is always a better tactic than negotiation.

The Kennedy administration was also the first to authorize surveillance of domestic political dissidents. The FBI, since the Roosevelt administration, had informally kept tabs on individuals thought to be a threat to national security. In the 1950s the FBI even launched the COINTEL program to disrupt the American Communist Party. But it was the Kennedy administration that authorized the FBI to use electronic surveillance to monitor the activities of civil rights leader Martin Luther King Jr. without securing a warrant.[17]

The Imperial Presidency continued to grow under Lyndon Johnson. In April of 1965, Johnson sent American troops to the Dominican Republic to prevent dissident military officers from taking power. Besides a disingenuous claim that he was acting to protect American lives, Johnson also falsely added that he was acting to prevent "communist conspirators" from setting up "another communist government in the Western Hemisphere."[18] There was in fact no evidence of Communist involvement. But Johnson's most famous misstatement of fact involved an alleged incident that was used to persuade Congress to pass the Gulf of Tonkin Resolution that authorized the Vietnam War. In June of 1964, Johnson announced in a televised speech that North Vietnamese ships had made an unprovoked attack on American navy ships in international waters off the coast of North Vietnam and that in retaliation he was ordering the bombing of sites in North Vietnam. Historians now believe that there was no such attack; it is also questionable whether the American ships were in international waters. Certainly Johnson knew such an attack was not unprovoked since the American ships were there to support South Vietnamese raids on North Vietnamese territory. Still, Johnson's version of events was unchallenged and provided the motivation for Congress to pass the Gulf of Tonkin Resolution that granted the president broad authority to use military force against North Vietnam.[19] Another clear example of Johnson's disregard for "checks and balances" was the secret war the CIA fought in Laos, a war continued under Richard Nixon.[20] It started as a small, CIA covert action but eventually mushroomed into a full-scale war in which 250 CIA officers led a secret army of forty thousand Hmong tribesmen against leftist Pathet Lao guerrilas.

President Johnson also used national security concerns to justify his decision to dramatically expand the government's surveillance and harassment of domestic political opponents in violation of the First and Fourth Amendments. Going well beyond the tactics that the Kennedy administration had used on Martin Luther King Jr., Johnson ordered that the FBI, CIA, and army investigate possible foreign connections to all organizations involved in either civil rights or anti–Vietnam War dissent Although the fact that there were no such connections was quickly established, government agents in the later 1960s continued to employ a wide variety of "dirty tricks" to monitor, harass, intimidate, and disrupt the protected constitutional activities of hundreds of thousands of American citizens.[21]

But it was Richard Nixon who (in Arthur Schlesinger Jr.'s words) "stripped away the fig leaves that his predecessor had draped over his assertion of unilateral presidential power."[22] Johnson had always buttressed his actions with claims of congressional consent like the Gulf of Tonkin Resolution. But when Nixon announced the American invasion of Cambodia in 1970, he rested his authority squarely on his duty as commander-in-chief "to protect the lives of American men."[23] Nixon not only continued the secret war in Laos but also initiated long-scale secret bombing of neutral Cambodia. And Nixon combined the use of independent presidential power and government secrecy with the power of presidential speech. At the same time Nixon was thus secretly broadening military actions in Southeast Asia, he continually assured the American public that he was winding the war down.

Nixon also expanded Johnson's illegal surveillance to include spying on journalists and the creation of an "enemies list" of political opponents to be targeted for government retaliation. The Nixon administration even engaged in burglaries to obtain political intelligence.[24] One break-in into the offices of the Democratic National Committee (DNC) in the Watergate complex in Washington, D.C., resulted in the Watergate scandal. Nixon responded to reports of his administration's involvement in the Watergate break-in by orchestrating a cover-up that included an order that the CIA lie to the American people by claiming that the break-in was part of a national security operation. When later asked about this unparalleled record of presidential law breaking, Nixon gave an answer that makes no sense from a "check and balances" perspective but that antici-pated the actions of future presidents: "When the President does it, that means it is not illegal."[25]

The Watergate scandal appeared to end the Imperial Presidency. News-paper reports of the illegalities of the Nixon administration put the presi-dency on the defensive. Finally he was forced to resign his office in dis-grace. The Democratic-controlled Congress felt it was necessary to return the presidency to a less independent role. To that end Congress, over Nixon's veto, passed the War Powers Resolution, which limited the presi-dent's power to involve U.S. troops in major combat actions to no more than sixty days without congressional authorization. Later Congress also passed the Foreign Intelligence Surveillance Act (FISA),[26] which required the CIA to obtain a judicial warrant before engaging in electronic eaves-dropping in the United States. So too the Freedom of Information Act (FOIA)[27] was amended to give the public access to more information in the possession of the government. Congress also passed legislation requiring the president to keep newly created intelligence committees in each house fully informed about all secret activities. Finally, Congress also provided for the appointment of special independent prosecutors to investigate and prosecute violations of law by executive officials, thereby removing the de facto immunity created by any attorney general's natural reluctance to prosecute members of his or her own administration.

Jimmy Carter now has a well-earned public image as a peacemaker in his role as former president. But the fact is that Carter signed off on almost as many covert-action orders as Nixon,[28] including an order to supply the rebels attempting to overthrow the pro-Soviet government in Afghanistan. That decision, made without congressional authority, proved to be a momentous one. The Soviets then invaded Afghanistan, a deci-sion that in turn motivated the CIA to shuffle even more aid to the reb-els, who eventually forced the Soviets out. Unfortunately, this victory over the Soviets also engendered the rise to power of a group of rebels who had been recipients of American aid—the Taliban, who have wreaked so much damage on American interests ever since.

But it was the election of Ronald Reagan that revived a truly aggres-sive stance on presidential powers over national security. Reagan not only continued the aid to the Afghan rebels but also had no qualms about ordering U.S. troops to invade the small Caribbean island nation of Gre-nada without consulting Congress. Of course, American presidents had independently authorized small-scale invasions like Grenada before. The more challenging issue was whether the president could act in the national security field in defiance of congressional will. Jackson's concurrence in *Youngstown* clearly said no, but Reagan took a different position. The theoretical issue became concrete when Reagan decided to overthrow the elected leftist government in Nicaragua by funding a secret CIA-created army, knows as the "Contras." The issue was joined when Congress passed legislation that categorically banned any American aid to the Contras.

The Reagan administration responded with a secret plan that not only permitted continued support of the Contras but also promised to solve another Reagan foreign policy headache: the fact that Shiite militias in Lebanon were holding seven Americans hostage. The Reagan administration would sell missiles to the new revolutionary Islamist government in Iran, who would in turn use its influence with the Shiite militias in Lebanon to secure release of the hostages. The sale price of the missiles would be inflated so as to produce surplus funds that the United States would then secretly funnel to the Contras. Secrecy was necessary on more than one account. First, Reagan had pledged never to negotiate with terrorists, and the hostage deal clearly violated that pledge. Secondly, the use of the revenues to support the Contras was a clear violation of the congressional ban. When the facts of the "Iran/Contra" deal became public, President Reagan's first reaction was to dissemble. ("We did not—repeat—did not trade weapons or anything else for hostages.")[29] But televised congressional hearings made clear not only that there had been a weapons-for-hostages deal but also that the clandestine aid had been provided to the Contras in violation of the congressional ban.

A bipartisan congressional report blasted the Reagan administration for indulging in acts Congress had prohibited, in violation of the separation-of-power principles set out in Justice Jackson's *Youngstown* concurrence. Its report concluded that the Reagan administration had done more than break a law; it had "undermined a cardinal principle of the constitution . . . that the president can spend money on a program only if he can convince congress to appropriate funds."[30] But a minority report written by a group of Republican legislators, including future vice-president Dick Cheney, came to a different conclusion. The minority report rejected the majority's conclusion that Reagan had acted beyond his constitutional powers, arguing instead that the legislation banning aid to the Contras itself unconstitutionally infringed upon the president's authority in the areas of foreign policy and national security. It concluded that congressional actions that interfere with the president's foreign policy powers should be looked at with skepticism: "if they interfere with core presidential foreign policy functions, they should be struck down."[31] The minority report, little noticed at the time, turned out to be the intellectual seed from which the National Security Presidency challenge to the official interpretation of presidential power would grow.

The first President Bush also had expansive views of presidential power, but he preferred to frame public statements in less absolute terms than Nixon or Reagan. Bush Sr. obtained congressional authorization before launching the Desert Storm campaign after Iraq's invasion of Kuwait. He did this after mounting an extremely sophisticated media campaign against Iraq that gave the Congress very little political choice. And while he wanted congressional support, he never said he needed it to act.

It is important that we understand President Clinton's record on presidential powers in national security affairs. Many commentators tend to associate expansive claims of presidential powers with Republican presidents like Nixon, Reagan, and the second Bush. The innuendo is that the problem would disappear with a Democratic president. This view ignores the expansive use of presidential power by Truman, Kennedy, and Johnson. And while President Clinton was less bellicose in his rhetoric than his Republican counterparts, he also continued the drift towards more presidential power on national security issues. Clinton independently approved the first CIA "rendition" program that snatched up people from one country for torturelike questioning in other countries.[32] Clinton also approved the use of military force in Bosnia, Haiti, and Kosovo without congressional authorization. He continued the Kosovo bombing even after the House of Representatives (in a tie vote) refused to authorize it.[33] Even though the Clinton administration had more qualms in theory about the use of presidential power, Jack Goldsmith fairly concludes that regardless of the president's party, "on matters of war and national security, institutional imperatives and precedents almost always prevailed."[34]

The Challenger

Up until 9/11/01, presidents were willing to formally work within the structure of the Jackson concurrence in *Youngstown*. That opinion's vague language gave presidents a good deal of what we might call "wiggle room." A president could always claim that Congress had indeed approved his act in some prior legislation. And, if Congress had not granted authority, the Jackson opinion also granted the president an undefined residuum of independent authority. These arguments were buttressed by the reassuring fact that federal courts were reluctant to accept cases involving national security and therefore unlikely to reject a president's argument. But during the presidency of George W. Bush, presidential claims that were implicit became explicit (albeit only in secret documents). It was the 9/11 attacks that permitted the National Security Presidency challenger to fully blossom.

Although foreign affairs issues were hardly mentioned in the 2000 presidential campaign, we know now that President George W. Bush had a clear foreign affairs agenda when he entered the White House. Part of that agenda, reflecting the beliefs of Vice-President Dick Cheney, included a halt to the "erosion" of presidential powers that had taken place after Watergate. In fact, Bush intended to do more than stop the erosion; he intended to advance the power of the presidency as an institution—to leave the presidency stronger than he found it. In January of 2001, almost nine months before 9/11, he told his national security team that he had three foreign policy objectives: get rid of Saddam Hussein, end American involvement in the Israeli-Palestinian peace process, and bring friendly governments to power in the Mideast.[35]

Bush made clear that he believed he had independent authority to make war. After the 9/11 attacks Congress almost unanimously authorized the president to "use all necessary and appropriate force against nations, organizations, or persons" who committed or supported the 9/11 attacks. While Bush thanked Congress for their expression of support, he did not feel he needed any congressional permission to attack Afghanistan. Bush had good authority from the Justice Department's Office of Legal Counsel (OLC) that reassured him on that point. The OLC is a little known but very powerful player in executive branch politics; it has the authority to issue legal opinions that are binding throughout the executive branch. It had issued just such a memo declaring that the Constitution gave the president inherent power, independent of Congress, to use force as he saw fit to protect American interests. The memo said that Bush not only had power to act without congressional authorization; he was also constitutionally immune from any limits Congress might attempt to impose on such a war. The memo concluded that Congress cannot "place any limits on the President's determinations as to any terrorist threat, the amount of military force to be used in response, or the method, timing, and nature of the response."[36] The memo was immediately classified as secret.

Another OLC memo concerned the secret executive order Bush signed authorizing the National Security Agency to eavesdrop on individuals suspected of terrorist-related activities in the United States. As we mentioned earlier, the Foreign Intelligence Surveillance Act (FISA) set up a procedure that the executive branch must follow to get a warrant for domestic national-security spying, a procedure the executive order said the NSA could ignore. This OLC memo, also secret, ruled that the executive order was within the president's constitutional powers because Congress had no power to restrict the president's chosen means of acquiring "battlefield intelligence," and the battlefield in the War on Terror extended to American soil. As the memo's author, John Yoo, explained, "I think there's a law greater than FISA, which is the constitution, and part of the constitution is the president's commander-in-chief power. Congress can't take away the president's powers in running war."[37]

Bush also claimed the right to terminate American treaty obligations without congressional consent. The president announced withdrawal from the Anti-Ballistic Missile (ABM) Treaty signed by President Nixon and ratified by the Senate in 1972. While Article II makes clear that the president and the Senate share the power to enter into treaties, the text of the Constitution is silent on the issue of terminating treaties. Logic would seem to argue that if both the president and Congress must be involved in entering a treaty, both should be involved in terminating it. If the president cannot autonomously terminate a law he disfavors, neither can he terminate a treaty he disfavors. But modern presidents have disagreed. The issue even reached the Supreme Court in the late 1970s, but the Court avoided ruling on the issue.[38] Bush simply announced withdrawal from the ABM Treaty on his own authority. The Republican-controlled Congress remained silent.

Another example of the National Security Presidency in action was Bush authorizing the CIA to use "aggressive" interrogation techniques (like "waterboarding") while questioning terrorist suspects. This authorization created two sets of legal problems. First, the Convention against Torture (CAT), to which the United States is a party, forbids both torture and "cruel, inhuman, and degrading treatment"; most commentators believe that some of the approved methods at least constituted the latter form of illegal conduct and perhaps the former. But administration officials were more worried about a second problem: a congressional statute implementing the convention makes it a felony to intentionally engage in torture, which the statute defined as acts "specifically intended to inflict severe physical or mental pain or suffering" upon a person held in custody.[39] While the CIA agents who would conduct the interrogations were not too worried about violating an international treaty like the Convention against Torture, they did fear prosecution for violation of a congressional statute carrying up to a twenty-year prison sentence.

Once again, the Office of Legal Counsel came to the rescue with one more secret memo that argued for a narrow reading of the statute forbidding torture. But then the memo went on to make a more controversial constitutional claim: the congressional statute was inoperative with regard to the interrogations because as commander-in-chief the president had authority to use whatever techniques he deemed necessary, even if they violated a statute. The memo concluded that "[j]ust as statutes that order the President to conduct warfare in a certain manner or for specific goals would be unconstitutional, so too are laws that seek to prevent the president from gaining the intelligence he believes necessary to prevent attacks upon the United States."[40]

President Bush would also issue "signing statements" in which he would announce his power to ignore certain provisions of congressional statutes as being in violation of his constitutional powers. Senator John McCain introduced legislation to make "acts constituting cruel, inhuman, or degrading treatment" illegal under American domestic law, as well as violations of the international convention. This legislation would make use of interrogation techniques like waterboarding a felony. The Bush administration strenuously opposed McCain's legislation, but the president announced he would sign it when it passed both houses of Congress with a veto-proof majority. He did sign the bill, but quietly afterward issued a "signing statement" that declared that the executive branch would construe the legislation "in a manner consistent with the constitutional authority of the President as Commander-in-Chief and consistent with constitutional limits on the judicial power. . . ."[41] In other words, the president would honor the statute only to the degree he cared to do so.

I think that we must concede that at least on the level of clarity the National Security Presidency is an improvement over the official interpretation it challenges. It articulates a comprehensive constitutional vision to justify the national security powers it claims. While much of this vision was set out in secret OLC memos, many of these memos have now become public, and their reasoning is open to public scrutiny. Also, the primary author of the memos, John Yoo, a respected legal academic, has explained the vision in law journal articles and a book.[42] And Jack

Goldsmith, another law professor who was head of the OLC during part of the Bush administration, has also written a book in which he sets out the constitutional views of Vice-President Dick Cheney. It turns out that Cheney's views (he is not a lawyer) were in large part developed by his long-time top legal aide, David Addington. Addington not only authored the constitutional analysis in the House minority report on the Iran-Contra affair; he also played a major role in forging the legal arguments that underlay Bush's claims to limitless power.[43]

When we look at the OLC memos, Yoo's books and articles, and the views of Cheney and Addington as set out in Professor Goldsmith's book, we see two mutually supporting lines of constitutional analysis. The first I identify with Yoo; it argues that, contrary to the conventional wisdom on the issue, the authors of the Constitution intended to lodge almost all power over foreign affairs and war and peace in the presidency. Placing powers of war and peace in the executive branch was the British constitutional model, and Yoo argues that the same arrangement was adopted by the framers of our Constitution. They accomplished this task by the first sentence of Article II, Section 1, which cryptically states, "The executive Power shall be vested in a President of the United States of America." Yoo argues that this vesting of the executive power (the "vesting clause") in the president was intended to give him all the power over foreign affairs enjoyed by the British king except those powers expressly allocated to Congress under Article I.[44] At the same time that Yoo gives an expansive reading to the vesting clause of Article II, he gives a narrow reading of Congress's power under Article I to "declare war," seeing it as no more than the formal right to declare the legal status of a war the executive has already commenced.[45] And as we have seen in the memos Yoo wrote while at the OLC, he believes not only that the president has power to commence wars but that any attempts by Congress to limit his war policies are themselves unconstitutional as a violation of his Article II powers. When critics argue that this enormous grant of power to the president violates our Constitution's commitment to checks and balances, Yoo points to Congress's power to refuse to appropriate funds to support a war they oppose. Of course, Professor Yoo knows that this happens to be a weapon that modern Congresses find politically impossible to invoke once American troops are committed.

According to Professor Goldsmith, David Addington relies primarily on the commander-in-chief power to justify his equally expansive view of presidential power. Addington, citing the practice of Abraham Lincoln during the Civil War, argues that the president has broad authority as commander-in-chief during a time of emergency to fulfill his constitutional oath to "preserve, protect, and defend the Constitution of the United States."[46] The commander-in-chief power gives the president power not only to act independently of Congress but also to keep his actions secret; and he can also ignore congressional limits on his choice of means to fulfill his broad duties as commander-in-chief. Here Addington goes well beyond what Lincoln claimed for the president. Lincoln made his acts public and conceded Congress's power to countermand them.

Yoo argues that his interpretation of Article II is faithful to the authors' original design. Limiting constitutional interpretation to the "original intent" of the framers has been a central tenet of American conservative constitutional dogma since the 1970s, when it was employed to attack "activist" Supreme Court decisions like *Roe v. Wade*. Whether or not "original intent" makes sense as a matter of constitutional theory, it is certainly difficult to square with American constitutional history since the Supreme Court has routinely adopted interpretations of the text not envisioned by its authors. One example is the First Amendment, a text that we will see in chapter 2 has been interpreted more expansively than its original intent would permit. And Yoo's expansive views of presidential power are also at variance with the way most scholars see the intent of the framers on that issue. If the framers did indeed intend to grant the president the same foreign affairs powers enjoyed by the British king, it was the best kept secret in American constitutional history. As Arthur M. Schlesinger Jr. makes clear, the framers certainly did not want to follow the British monarchy as a model for the presidency. "As victims of what they considered a tyrannical royal prerogative, they were determined to fashion for themselves a Presidency that would be strong, but still limited."[47] Addington's theory also seems difficult to square with original intent since, whatever the merit of his views, Lincoln was not one of the framers and read into the text emergency powers they had not included.

But I do not think we should reject the National Security Presidency on the basis that it is not consistent with the "original intent" of the document's authors. Like most constitutional commentators, I think that to do so would overstate the importance of the authors' original intent in constitutional interpretation. It is one relevant factor, but there are other factors that also should be considered in interpreting the Constitution. We should also look to the goals of the constitutional enterprise, the structure of the text, later Supreme Court interpretations, and the present and future consequences of proposed interpretations. I am especially influenced by the first and last of these criteria. I think we should ask ourselves whether the National Security Presidency best furthers the Constitution's goals in our own day.

Let's first attempt to state the case for the National Security Presidency in a sympathetic manner. A supporter might argue as follows: The border between the conduct of foreign policy that all concede is placed in the president's hands and the use of military force is too murky to delineate clearly; sometimes force or the credible threat of force is necessary to effectuate foreign policy goals. Only the president has full access to the information necessary to take successful action in the foreign policy area, and the need to keep diplomatic and military planning secret prevents him from sharing that information with Congress and the public. For this reason, the president is the only elected official who can, as it were, see the whole foreign policy playing field. So too the president is the only official elected by all the people, and therefore he has a special democratic claim to make decisions for the whole nation. He has the right to make the decisions he feels are necessary to defend the nation, and if his decisions prove wrong, the voters can withdraw that authority at the next election. And, in the interim, the Congress always retains authority to deprive the president of funds to implement policies they disapprove of. And if sometimes the president's national security responsibilities will require him to curtail individual statutory and constitutional rights, this is a small price to pay to protect the security that is a prerequisite for the existence of those rights. As Judge Posner reminds us, the Constitution, after all, is not a suicide pact.[48]

The idea of an all-powerful leader protecting the nation in times of peril is seductive, but also dangerous. The remainder of this book argues that the National Security Presidency fails to measure up on two fundamental constitutional metrics. It incorporates an unduly thin conception of democratic government, and it fails to provide an effective structure for making national security decisions.

With regard to democratic government, the National Security Presidency reduces democratic control to the holding of a plebiscite on foreign policy every four years. While it is true that the president and vice-president are the only candidates who stand before the whole nation for election, the genius of our Constitution is to recognize the value of a plurality of overlapping electorates, each contributing to decisions on war and peace. Candidates for different offices face different electorates and serve for different terms. Obviously, the smaller the electorate, the larger impact the individual voter has within in it, a fact that calls for the House of Representatives to play a significant role. So the Senate is structured to give geographic regions of the nation effective voice, and they also should be heard. And the First Amendment assures that even groups who are not powerful enough to elect their candidates will be allowed to have their voices heard. The democratic pedigree of such a multilayered system is much better than that of a single election every four years.

And upon reflection, even the argument that the voters authorize a president's national security policy every four years is more rhetoric than fact. Even if we preferred a four-year plebiscite on national security policy, presidential elections rarely perform that function. Presidents Johnson and Nixon actually presented themselves as "peace" candidates just before initiating and expanding the Vietnam War. And foreign policy was almost never mentioned in the 2000 campaign that elected George W. Bush, who led us into the Iraq quagmire.

History also shows that the campaign for reelection of a sitting president who has involved us in a major war is dramatically skewed by voters' reluctance to signal any lack of support for troops in the field, no matter how misguided they may feel the war itself is. Most of the voting public was disenchanted with the Vietnam War in 1968, but the war continued until 1975. So too most of the public felt by 2004 that the Iraq War had been a mistake, but that didn't prevent President Bush from winning reelection on the basis of "stay the course" rhetoric We can only speculate about the reasons why Bush was able to be reelected while Johnson was forced from office. I would suggest that two contributing reasons were that Bush made more effective use of the power of presidential speech than did Johnson; and the Warren Court was more protective of First Amendment activities opposing Johnson's war than the Rehnquist or Roberts Courts were after 9/11.

Arguments for expanded presidential power assume that we always face a necessary choice between more democratic involvement and greater efficiency in attaining foreign policy goals. More democratic checks on presidential power lead to less effective policies. Presidents believe that only they know what must be done and how to do it. But again history shows that democratic checks on presidential power, supported by First Amendment rights, often yields better substantive decisions than a process dominated by the president. A richer debate, involving more perspectives, better weighs the pros and cons of military involvement than one dominated by executive branch group think. Certainly we would have been better served by a full, informed discussion of the reasons to invade Iraq and the possible consequences of the invasion than we were by the fear-driven debate dominated by presidential rhetoric that actually took place. And, while it may be true that some individual rights must sometimes be sacrificed to some degree in favor of national security concerns, this is usually not the case with free speech rights. Dissenting speech that alerts us to the weakness of government proposals makes us more rather than less safe.

We should also recognize the impossibility of disentangling national security affairs from the other areas of governmental responsibility. Concentrating national security power in the president inevitably has effects on other areas. When a president leads us into a war, this not only has foreign policy repercussions; it also expends funds that might otherwise have been used for other governmental purposes like health care. And curtailing individual rights in the name of national security leads to curtailment of rights in other contexts. We start with an elected dictator in the area of foreign affairs and end with just an elected dictator.

The reader may well want to know the current status of the National Security Presidency challenger. The reassuring news is that it's still only the challenger. When the Bush administration argued that the president had authority without congressional consent to designate individuals as enemy combatants, the Court refused to accept this argument.[49] But the Court passed up the chance to reject the president's argument as an erroneous interpretation of his powers. Instead the justices decided the case on narrower grounds. So the claim to independent power is still in play for future cases. On the other hand, it is reassuring to note that the Court has rejected the extreme claim that the president is not limited by congressional statutes in the national security area.[50] But, as we will see in chapter 6, the Court's penchant to rule narrowly on the facts of each case and its use of technical doctrines, like standing, that make it difficult for plaintiffs to challenge presidential actions in the federal courts have resulted in the National Security Presidency operating as the de facto Constitution over a wide array of issues. So long as the courts don't reject the theory outright, presidents can continue to use it to guide their actions, safe in the knowledge that a contradictory court ruling is unlikely to materialize. And while President Obama has made it clear that he will not continue many of the most controversial national security policies of the Bush administration, he has not renounced the power to adopt any policies he feels will advance national security interests. So I think the most prudent conclusion to make of the status of the National Security Presidency is that, while not triumphant, it remains alive and well to fight future battles.

※ 2 *※*

The Manufacture of Consent

Naturally the common people don't want war; neither in Russia nor in England nor in America, nor for that matter in Germany. That is understood. But after all it is the leaders of the country who determine the policy and it is always a simple matter to drag the people along. . . . That is easy. All you have to do is tell them they are being attacked and denounce the pacifists for lack of patriotism and exposing the country to danger. It works the same way in any country. —Hermann Goering

While chapter 1 discussed the president's power to act in the national security context, this chapter focuses on the power of presidential speech in the area of national security. It turns out that the power of speech is just as potent a weapon in the president's arsenal as the power to act. But while the scope of the president's power to act has been the subject of much constitutional debate, there has been no similar discussion of the constitutional dimensions of the power of presidential speech. There have been no Supreme Court decisions and no spirited debates in law reviews. But beneath this silence lurks a dark fact: the power of presidential speech corrupts our national security debates.

For supporters of the National Security Presidency, the ability of the president to use all the rhetorical tools at his disposal to mold public opinion is an essential part of his job. It was for this reason that President Ronald Reagan was affectionately known as the Great Communicator. But from a larger democratic perspective, the influence of presidential speech on national security decisions is more problematic. Of course, no one doubts that the president must be able to communicate effectively on national security issues in order to make his case to the American people.

But he is able to do much more than make his case; he dominates the discussion.

A variety of factors combine to create this domination. The president not only has unequaled access to the media; he also controls most of the information relevant to national security discussions. Furthermore, he can not only direct government agencies to disrupt political opponents but also take actions (like committing American troops) that preempt later policy debates Perhaps most importantly, the president's symbolic position as national leader grants his speech on national security affairs special authority. All these factors combine to allow him to drown out competing voices.

Unfortunately, awareness that presidential speech threatens democratic values does not automatically yield a satisfactory solution to the problem it presents. The case against presidential propaganda roughly parallels that against unlimited campaign spending.[1] In each case, a necessary component of the political process, good in itself, becomes dangerous because it gives disproportionate influence to some speakers. Financial contributions are necessary to campaigns; it is only when one group of citizens through large contributions gains disproportionate influence that restrictions are necessary to even the political playing field. Presidential speech is a similar phenomenon. It's a necessary part of democratic debate that only becomes dangerous when it permits presidents to overwhelm competing voices. But while limits on the amount of campaign spending are possible, it is difficult to imagine a limit on the amount of presidential speech. We cannot limit the number of times the president speaks nor censor his choice of message.

Presidential speech is a part of the larger issue of government propaganda that has bedeviled democracy since the beginning of the twentieth century. Still, we can take steps to counteract its distorting impact; the rest of this book is an attempt to do just that.

The Rhetorical Presidency

But before we discuss responses to the danger presented by presidential speech, perhaps we should first trace the history of how it became the problem it now is. We saw in chapter 1 that the authors of the Constitution intended to create a presidency with substantial powers, but these powers were primarily defensive in nature, designed to complement and limit those of the more powerful Congress. The president was to execute laws Congress would pass; negotiate treaties the Senate would ratify; manage wars Congress would declare. The president was also assigned additional powers, mostly defensive in nature, like a qualified veto over legislation he thought imprudent and the power (subject to Senate approval) to appoint judges and high executive officers.

No one foresaw the political colossus the presidency would become by the late twentieth century. And certainly no one foresaw that this preeminence would stem in large part from the power of presidential speech. The framers would have been alarmed as well as surprised by the later historical turn of events. They saw the direct appeal of a popular leader to mass opinion as a danger to constitutional government and attempted to design institutions that would prevent it. The *Federalist Papers* begin with the warning that "of those men who have overturned the liberties of republics, the greatest have begun their career by paying obsequious court to the people, commencing demagogues and ending tyrants."[2] The two times when presidential speech is mentioned in the Constitution both reflect its secondary role in policy formation.[3] The veto power says that if the president decides to veto a bill, he should return it "with his objections" to Congress.[4] And Article II, Section 3 provides that the president "shall from time to time give to the congress information of the State of the Union, and recommend to their Consideration such Measures as he shall judge necessary and expedient." Both texts see the president's role as secondary to that of the Congress, and both explicitly require that he address his message to Congress and not appeal directly to public opinion.

Early constitutional practice reflected this restrained view of the proper role of presidential speech. George Washington set the tone in his first inaugural speech. Washington refused to discuss policy. Instead, he used the opportunity to praise virtue and display his own excellent character. So too throughout the nineteenth century, presidential messages to Congress, including the State of the Union speech, were written documents addressed to Congress. Both the fact that they were addressed to Congress and the fact that they were in written form provided protection against the temptation to appeal to popular passion. Speeches to the public, like Lincoln's Gettysburg Address, tended to be more ceremonial than policy oriented in nature.

Theodore Roosevelt was the first president to explore the power of presidential rhetoric addressed over the heads of Congress to the people. He used the "bully pulpit" of the presidency to sell his policies to the public, who in turn pressured members of Congress to support them. But, it was Woodrow Wilson who brought the "rhetorical presidency" to maturity. Wilson, a political scientist by profession, believed that the presidency had been too subservient to Congress during the nineteenth century. Wilson pointed out that, instead of the calm policy discussions the framers hoped for in Congress, legislation was in fact too often the product of political-party and interest-group wrangling. He felt that the system lacked the necessary political energy to see that the democratic will of the majority was honored and that it was the role of the president as the nation's leader to provide that energy. Wilson argued that the primary source of the president's power came not from his narrowly prescribed constitutional duties but from the fact that he was the only official elected by all the people. Only the president could claim to speak for all the people. Therefore, it was his duty to first determine and then express the people's will. And Wilson believed that both in determining and in expressing the national will the president must take an active and creative role.

Wilson pioneered what he called the "visionary speech." It required the leader to listen to all the discordant voices of society and unite them into a "single vision" so that he could articulate "the common meaning of the common voice."[5] Wilson's speeches while in office reflected this activist view of presidential rhetoric. He replaced the nineteenth-century tradition of the State of the Union address as a written message to Congress with the modern practice of a spoken speech formally addressed to the Congress but in reality directed towards the general public. He was also the first president to engage in full-time speaking tours during his campaigns. Jeffrey Tulis concludes that under Wilson the goal of presidential rhetoric was to "find the appeal to passion that would activate popular opinion, intensify it, bring it to expression."[6]

The Wilson administration's use of speech in persuading the American people to enter World War I is an excellent example of the influence presidential speech can have on national security issues. It was not an easy sell. America and Americans had traditionally shown little interest in European politics, and Wilson's earlier policy of "neutrality" was very popular. In fact, he was reelected in 1916 on a platform that took credit for "keeping us out of war." And important groups of Americans had ethnic loyalties to different European nations involved in the war that made American involvement a very divisive political issue. In divining a "single vision" out of this mélange of isolationism and ethnic division, Wilson appealed to the public's patriotic belief that America was morally superior to the decadent Europeans. Consider this section of Wilson's message calling for America's entry into the war:

> We have no selfish ends to serve. We desire no conquest, no dominion. We seek no indemnities for ourselves, no material compensation for the sacrifices we shall freely make. We are but one of the champions of mankind. We shall be satisfied when those rights have been made as secure as the faith and the freedom of nations can make them.[7]

The goal of these lofty sentiments lay not in setting out and analyzing facts surrounding American involvement in the war but rather in using presidential rhetoric to (in the *Federalist*'s phrase) "pay obsequious court" to the people in order to manipulate public opinion.

Wilson's administration pioneered the use of sophisticated methods of mass persuasion in American politics. Soon after war was declared, Wilson created the Committee on Public Information (CPI) to sell the war to the American public. The CPI not only echoed Wilson's patriotic themes but also added a darker subtext. The committee's chairman, George Creel, later clearly described the committee's goals:

> What we had to have was no mere surface unity, but a passionate belief in the justice of America's cause that should weld the people of the United States in a white-hot mass instinct with fraternity, devotion, courage, and deathless determination.[8]

This "white-hot mass instinct" was to be molded in part by appeals to conscious and unconscious fears and prejudices. And note also that Creel was aiming not for majority support but for unanimity. There was no room for dissent. The government allocated large amounts of money and personnel to the committee's operations. The committee produced 75 million pamphlets explaining America's war aims and enlisted 75,000 speakers to give 755,000 government-authored prowar speeches across the country. It also issued countless posters advertising the war and 200,000 still photos dramatizing it.

While sometimes the CPI spoke in Wilson's lofty phrases, often it preferred to appeal to xenophobia and prejudice. One striking example was the CPI's popular "Halt the Hun" poster. The CPI portrayed the German kaiser in other government posters, in the words of one commentator, as "hollow-eyed, despicable with cringing bravado, his hands bloody, the mark of Cain on his forehead."[9] CPI spokesman Carl Vrooman reflected this xenophobic approach in a highly popular speech that Creel himself said he had read "with joy and profit":

> We are in a crusade not only for liberty and democracy but for a peace that must never again be jeopardized by the crazy dreams of world conquest of a war-mad Kaiser surrounded by a war-mad conclave of Hindenburgs, Ludenddorffs, Tirpitzes, and Crown Princes. We mean to demonstrate so that a thousand years from now people will read, and rejoice in the fact, that in our generation, civilized nations by the use of civilized methods were able to defend themselves against terrorism, Tirpitzism, Zepellinism, and the blood-red Moloch of materialism.[10]

It was only after the war hysteria ended that commentators began to reflect on the tension between the Wilson administration's management of public opinion and fundamental tenets of democratic government. The highly respected political commentator Walter Lippman pointed out that while democratic theory saw policy percolating upwards from the views of independent citizens, the new political reality was that policy was increasingly formulated top-down by elites who used the techniques of mass persuasion to achieve what Lippman termed the "manufacture of consent."[11]

War propaganda has been a staple of American political life ever since. During World War I, its practitioners did not shy away from the term "propaganda" to describe their work, but when the Nazis gave a negative connotation to that term in the 1930s, the preferred term became "public relations," though the techniques remained the same. All American presidents from Franklin Delano Roosevelt to George W. Bush have made sophisticated use of the power of presidential speech to secure popular support for their policies on foreign affairs.

Nixon's use of presidential rhetoric with regard to the Vietnam War is a good example of how powerful a tool it can be. During the 1968 presidential campaign Nixon assured the voters that he would "end the war and win the peace."[12] What he did not tell the American people was that his plan to end the war was to win it. Nixon's goal was the same one Johnson had when he expanded the war in 1965—an anti-Communist government in power in South Vietnam and the removal of North Vietnamese troops from the South.

Towards this goal Nixon took a series of actions to change the political image of the war. He called for an end to the draft in order to remove that easy target of antiwar sentiment. He also began to incrementally reduce American troop involvement in the war; he called this fateful step the "Vietnamization" of the war, implying that the South Vietnamese would now take responsibility for their own fate. While "Vietnamization" was successful in neutralizing political opposition to the war, it also severely limited Nixon's options in bringing about the resolution he wanted. He also tried to keep pressure on North Vietnam by keeping open the option of increased bombing even beyond the levels authorized by President Johnson. Nixon felt Johnson had been too timid in refusing to extend the bombing to Hanoi, Haiphong, and other heavily populated areas of North Vietnam. And Nixon initiated a secret bombing program of neutral Cambodia. Nixon even considered the use of nuclear weapons against North Vietnam to be an available option. At the same time that he threatened North Vietnam, Nixon also fostered a policy of "détente" towards the Soviet Union and an "opening" to Communist China, offering them diplomatic and trade benefits in hoped that they could rein in their fractious junior partner. And he continued and extended President Johnson's secret policy of spying on and harassing opponents of the war.

But Nixon's most effective tool was his use of the power of presidential speech to reconfigure the war in the public mind as a struggle for national dignity rather than military victory. Time and again Nixon addressed the American people from the Oval Office, stating his case in highly emotional language. An excellent example is a Nixon speech in November of 1969. Large antiwar demonstrations had taken place on October 15, and more were scheduled for November 15, but Nixon was able to use the demonstrations as a backdrop for his own nationally televised speech from the Oval Office on November 3 in which he appealed to America's "silent majority" to support him in his efforts to end the war. And he finished his plea for support with a veiled reference to his antiwar critics: "North Vietnam cannot defeat or humiliate the United States. Only Americans can do that."[13] The speech was an enormous political success. The White House switchboard was swamped with congratulatory phone calls, a response that had been orchestrated by the Republican Party officials. Support for Nixon's policy rose from 52 percent in October to 68 percent a few days after the speech. Nixon had played the patriotism card to persuade most Americans to support his policies. Nixon knew he had hit a home run. He told his aides, "We've got those liberal bastards on the run and we're going to keep them on the run."[14] And, for the most part, Nixon did just that until 1973 when he suffered the political consequences of the self-inflicted wounds of the Watergate scandal.

While Nixon was successful in maintaining public support for the war, he was not successful in his goal of maintaining a pro-American government in South Vietnam. The outcome that actually emerged in 1975 was essentially what the North Vietnamese had insisted on from the outset—a reunited Vietnam under Communist rule. And the consequences of defeat were not as injurious to American interests as Presidents Johnson and Nixon had predicted. Vietnam has never become a democracy, but now its leaders are much more interested in attracting Western capital than fomenting world revolution.

Let me be clear. I do not mean to imply that Nixon's use of emotional appeals to patriotism was improper. In fact, I admire his skillful use of presidential rhetoric. Presidents must be persuasive to fulfill their constitutional role. The problem is not that presidents are skillful speakers but that the special place they occupy in the American political system both as speakers and as actors allows them to distort the policy debate. Part of the problem is the president's unparalleled access to the media; another part is his ability to keep controversial actions secret. Both prevent opposing views from having the opportunity to get political traction. Democracy cannot work if a president can with great fanfare announce a reduction in American involvement in a war at the same time that he secretly expands bombing campaigns.

Selling the Invasion of Iraq

Nixon was neither the first nor the last president to make effective use of presidential speech in selling his national security policies to the public. The role of the rhetoric of President George W. Bush and his surrogates in persuading the American people that the United States should invade Iraq is a textbook example of the power of presidential speech. Although Bush never mentioned the possibility of invading Iraq during the 2000 presidential campaign, we know now that it was on his policy agenda when he took office in January 2001, well before the terrorist attacks on the World Trade Center. The overthrow of Saddam Hussein was discussed at the first meeting of the National Security Council in January of that year.[15] High administration officials saw the 9/11 attacks as creating a political opportunity to move on Iraq. For instance, in the days immediately after the attacks, Secretary of Defense Donald Rumsfeld argued that the American military response to 9/11 should include "getting Iraq."[16] Less than a week after 9/11, President Bush ordered the Pentagon to begin planning military options for the invasion of Iraq. Planning was stepped up after the quick victory in Afghanistan, and at the end of December 2001, General Tommy Franks delivered to Bush a preliminary plan for the invasion. Franks said that from a military perspective the invasion could begin as early as the spring of 2002.

But the invasion of Iraq had to wait until public support for it had been created. While Americans knew that Saddam had been our enemy in the Gulf War and was reported to be a cruel dictator, neither most experts nor the general public saw Iraq as an imminent danger to American national security. To change this political attitude, the Bush administration devised a media strategy with three interrelated objectives. The first was to portray Saddam Hussein, our recent ally, as the incarnation of evil like the German czar in World War I. Secondly, it was necessary to persuade the American people that Saddam presented a present threat to our national security because he possessed (or would soon possess) nuclear weapons that he would not hesitate to use against the United States. The third goal was to link the new idea of invading Iraq with the politically popular "War on Terror" against al-Qaeda.

Facts were readily available to support the claim that Saddam was a cruel dictator, although the evidence of his most heinous deeds related to past events. That Iraq was a present threat to the United States and that Saddam was linked to al-Qaeda were more difficult propositions to substantiate. The United Nations had destroyed Iraq's nuclear capability in the 1990s, and there was no reliable evidence either that it had restarted a nuclear program or, even if it had done so, that it had come close to building a nuclear bomb. And, as to the link with al-Qaeda, while Saddam and al-Qaeda shared a hostility towards the United States, the secularist Iraqi dictator had little sympathy with religious extremists like al-Qaeda who might prove a threat to his own rule.

The first salvo in the Bush campaign to invade Iraq was the president's State of the Union address in late January 2002. Addressing a nationwide television audience of fifty-two million people, Bush boldly declared that North Korea, Iran, and Iraq constituted an "axis of evil, arming to threaten the peace of the world. By seeking weapons of mass destruction, these regimes pose a grave and growing danger."[17] Bush intended the phrase "axis of evil" to linger in the minds of his listeners. From a factual perspective, the phrase seems an odd choice. It implies that North Korea, Iran, and Iraq were allies when they were not. Iran and Iraq, in fact, had fought a long, bloody war in the 1980s. But from a propaganda perspective, the phrase was a stroke of genius. The use of "evil" transformed the discussion from the realm of demonstrable fact to the realm of morality, where values and emotion reigned. It also echoed Ronald Reagan's famous reference to the Soviet Union as the "evil empire." And whatever its factual inaccuracy, the term "axis" psychologically linked the invasion of Iraq with the "good war" of World War II when America led its allies against the "axis" of Germany, Italy, and Japan. It also linked, at a symbolic level, North Korea, Iran, and Iraq with the members of that earlier "axis" that included the Nazis. And by adding North Korea and Iran to the "axis of evil," Bush was able to conceal that his actual military plans only involved the invasion of Iraq. But sophisticated listeners understood the speech's underlying message. *Washington Post* columnist Charles Krauthammer wrote, "Iraq is what this speech was about. This speech was just short of a declaration of war."[18]

The term "weapons of mass destruction" was also an artful choice. Supporters of the war pointed to two distinct dangers Iraq presented. The first was biological or chemical weapons; the second was a nuclear device. The evidence was stronger that Saddam might have poisonous gases that could be used against an enemy. Actually he had used them against his own people. But these did not constitute a grave threat to the United States thousands of miles away. The possession of a nuclear bomb would constitute a clear danger, but the evidence that Iraq had such a weapon was weak. By bringing both threats within the umbrella term "weapons of mass destruction," the president could conflate the more clear evidence of chemical and biological weapons with the greater danger of a nuclear device.

During the spring and summer of 2002, Bush kept the Iraq issue alive by making apparently impromptu remarks to the press. In April he told a British newsman, "I made my mind up that Saddam needs to go. . . . The worst thing that could happen would be to allow a nation like Iraq, run by Saddam Hussein, to develop weapons of mass destruction, and then team up with terrorist organizations so they can blackmail the world. I am not going to let that to happen."[19] In May, in an address to the midshipmen at

West Point, Bush introduced a moral justification for invasion of a nation that had not yet acted against America. Americans feel themselves to be a peace-loving nation that only responds to attacks. Engaging in an "offensive war" would transform us into aggressors. That's why President Johnson used what he claimed were unprovoked attacks by North Vietnam on American ships to jumpstart the Vietnam War. Since Saddam was not likely to attack us, a theory was needed to justify our attacking him. Bush called it "preemption." "The war on terror will not be won on the defensive. We must take the battle to the enemy, disrupt his plans, and confront the worst threats before they emerge."[20]

The press continued to print stories throughout the summer about rumors of various plans for war. Bush turned back questions about actual plans for war with the coy response, "I have no plans to attack on my desk."[21] In late August, Vice-President Cheney turned up the rhetorical heat in a fiery speech to the hawkish Veterans of Foreign Wars. Cheney omitted the carefully placed qualifiers that had been placed in Bush's speeches: "Deliverable weapons of mass destruction in the hands of a terror network, or a murderous dictator, or the two working together constitute as grave a threat as can be imagined. The risks of inaction are far greater than the risk of action."[22] "Simply stated, there is no doubt that Saddam Hussein now has weapons of mass destruction [and] there is no doubt that he is amassing them to use against our friends, against our allies and against us."[23] The press interpreted these bellicose statements as administration policy.

All this set the stage for the events of the fall. The administration's goal was to persuade Congress to grant the president the proverbial "blank check" to oust Saddam, including an invasion if necessary. The campaign also was geared to bring victory to the Republican candidates in the November 2002 midterm congressional elections. The kick-off to the fall campaign was planned for early September, after Bush returned from his vacation at his Texas ranch. A Bush chief aide jokingly justified the September date with the quip, "From a marketing point of view, you don't introduce new products in August."[24]

On Saturday, September 7, British Prime Minister Tony Blair was flown to Camp David for a one-day "summit" with President Bush. In answers to reporters, Bush said unequivocally that "Saddam possesses weapons of mass destruction." On Sunday morning an article by Judith Miller appeared in the New York Times with the headline "U.S. Says Hussein Intensifies Quest for A-Bomb Parts."[25] As it had done in the past, the

Bush administration used Miller and the *Times* as a conduit for the selective leaking of classified information; this time the meat of the story was an allegation by unnamed government sources of attempts by Saddam to purchase "specially designed aluminum tubes" that American officials believed were to be used as centrifuges to enrich uranium. In fact, this was old intelligence data that many in the CIA thought to be of dubious value (and that later proved to be untrue), but the sudden appearance of the story was a "news event" that provided concrete evidence supporting the administration's claims.

Having planted the story in the press, the administration then had high officials trumpet the importance of the *Times* discovery on the Sunday morning talk shows. Vice-President Cheney appeared on NBC; National Security Advisor Condoleezza Rice, on CNN; Secretary of State Colin Powell, on Fox; and Secretary of Defense Donald Rumsfeld, on CBS. Rumsfeld's comments were typical: "Imagine a September 11 with weapons of mass destruction."[26] But the sound bite (crafted by White House speech writers) that would echo through the coming months belonged to Rice: "We don't want the smoking gun to be a mushroom cloud."[27]

President Bush himself gave the campaign's keynote address on October 7, 2002, in Cincinnati. The speech was watched live by seventeen million Americans on the arch-conservative Fox TV network and was covered widely by the press and television for days after the speech. The timing of the speech was important. It was the week before Congress was going to take up the president's proposal for a resolution giving him a free hand, including the use of military force, to deal with Saddam and one month before the congressional midterm elections. Bush carefully laid out the case for ousting Saddam, making bold claims about how close Iraq was to getting a bomb: "The evidence indicates that Iraq is reconstituting its nuclear weapons program. . . . If the Iraqi regime is able to produce, buy, or steal an amount of highly enriched uranium a little larger than a softball, it could have nuclear weapons in less than a year."[28] Bush also linked Saddam to terrorism. "Iraq could decide on any given day to provide a biological or chemical weapon to a terrorist group or individual terrorists. Alliance with terrorists could allow the Iraqi regime to attack America without leaving any fingerprints."[29] The president then borrowed Secretary of State Rice's powerful mushroom cloud image. "Facing clear evidence of peril, we cannot wait for final proof—the smoking gun—that could come in the form of a mushroom cloud."[30]

In November, the Republicans won both the House and the Senate with large majorities and soon thereafter the Congress gave the president the blank check on Iraq he wanted. A few members of Congress attempted to stand against the rush to war, but no critic could get much traction in face of the administration's repeated claims that a murderous tyrant was close to achieving a nuclear capability that he would use, at a minimum, to blackmail America. By the end of October polls showed that not only did an overwhelming percentage of Americans support Bush on ousting Saddam but a surprising percentage believed that Saddam was connected to 9/11 attacks, a claim the Bush administration had never made.[31]

The campaign to sell the invasion of Iraq continued up to and even after the actual invasion in the spring of 2003. Highlights were Secretary of State Colin Powell's dramatic presentation to the United Nations Security Council and President Bush's 2003 State of the Union address, in which he reported that Iraq was close to achieving a nuclear capacity. We know now that much of the evidence Secretary of State Powell presented to the United Nations proved false. Time and again Powell drew categorical conclusions from evidence he knew was ambiguous in nature. Bush in his State of the Union address made a statement about Iraqi attempts to buy enriched uranium in Africa that he probably knew to be false. In fact, most of the evidence used by the administration to persuade the American people that Saddam presented an imminent threat to national security appears to have been either false or highly overblown in its purported significance. But the steady drumbeat of prowar propaganda drowned out evidence (like the failure of the UN inspectors to find evidence of an Iraqi nuclear program) inconsistent with the prowar thesis. Many potential critics were suspicious, but finally chose to remain silent rather than pay the political price of opposing an invasion that clearly was going to take place and promised to be militarily successful.

But by the time the public knew the true facts about Saddam and weapons of mass destruction, the invasion of Iraq was history and the insurrection it provoked in full bloom. But the collapse of the administration's original justification for the war had little effect on public support for the war because Bush deftly substituted a new propaganda narrative justifying the invasion—the creation of a democratic state in Iraq—for the discredited weapons-of-mass-destruction rationale. And so the public relations experts quickly transferred their efforts to the new campaign.

How Presidential Speech Threatens Democratic Debate

We face a paradox; presidential speech is both a necessary component of and a serious threat to democratic deliberation on national security issues. There is no way that the president can fulfill his constitutional duties under Article II without addressing the American people often and persuasively. Our democracy has evolved since 1787 and an activist president and direct presidential appeals to the public are now an integral part of our constitutional order. But recent history makes it impossible to ignore the fact that presidents can and do use their superior access to the media, their control of information, and the president's status as national leader to dominate the normal democratic decision-making process on issues relating to national security. The challenge is to devise a system that permits the president to persuasively make his case without overwhelming opposing voices.

But, first, we must be more precise in setting out how presidential speech constitutes a threat. The threat does not come from the fact that sometimes presidents make statements that prove to be false. As the Supreme Court said in *New York Times v. Sullivan*, "[E]rroneous statement is inevitable in free debate and [must] be protected if the freedoms of expression are to have the 'breathing space' that they 'need to survive.'"[32] Nor is the problem that presidents often choose to frame their messages in language that appeals to the passions more than the intellect. The Supreme Court in *Cohen v. California*[33] made clear that the emotional dimension of speech is just as much protected by the First Amendment as the ideas it communicates: If President Bush felt that he could best make his case for invading Iraq by warning Americans about smoking guns that might come in the form of a mushroom cloud, the First Amendment fully supports his right to do so.

The danger of presidential speech on national security issues comes from its quantity and the president's unique role in our political system. The president has many advantages not afforded any other speaker. For instance, no other speaker has anything close to the same access to the mass media that the president possesses. He not only is able to command a national audience at any time but can use administration officials and political allies to echo his chosen message. The study of propaganda has shown that simple messages repeated time and again are the most effective, and no other speaker is able to match the president's ability to accomplish the required degree of saturation.

His unrivaled access to the media also allows the president to set the agenda. If President Bush says there is an "axis of evil" that includes Iraq, the press dutifully reports his claim. If they can find a mainstream critic to publicly disagree with the president's assessment of Iraq, they will also report that fact. Often that is hard to do because mainstream politicians see little benefit from appearing to support a foreign dictator like Saddam Hussein. Furthermore, the press does not feel that objective reporting requires them to print the views of domestic critics outside the mainstream, nor to be "neutral" about whom to believe when there is a public dispute between the president and a foreign dictator. The press assumes that the president is telling the truth unless there is hard evidence otherwise. The executive branch's control of national security information usually makes such evidence unavailable. And as media expert Mark Hertsgaard points out, even when the media is willing to correct the president when it is shown that he has misspoken, its desire to be perceived as "neutral" makes it reluctant to do so often. So the president, corrected in print one time, may continue to repeat the contested comment without fear of further correction.[34]

And often the White House is able to intervene to prevent a critical story from being printed. For instance, after pleas from the White House, the *New York Times* decided not to print a story about the Kennedy administration's plan to invade the Bay of Pigs. So, too, after pleas by the Bush administration on national security grounds, the *Times* delayed reporting a story on the existence of the National Security Agency's secret program of spying on American citizens until after the 2004 presidential elections. One suspects that the *Times*, whose editorial page supported Bush's opponent John Kerry, feared that reporting the story would appear partisan.

Critical reporting is also chilled by the government's capacity to attack its critics. President Nixon's administration made express threats of retaliation against newspapers critical of its policies. But threats need not be so direct to be effective. Not only is there the threat of limiting access to the president and other high officials whom reporters need to talk to in order to do their jobs, but reporters are well aware that articles critical of the government will provoke angry calls from the White House to their editors alleging a lack of reportorial objectivity, a consequence that never follows a story sympathetic to the government's position.

The president also has the unique ability to determine to a large extent what facts are available for debate on national security issues. As we will see in chapter 4, the executive branch decides what information is classified on national security grounds and what information is not. As we saw in the run-up to the invasion of Iraq, classified information can also be declassified and/or leaked to the press when it suits the administration's political goals. The president can not only control what classified information is made public; he can also create new "facts" for use in the debate when displeased with the information he is receiving from normal channels. Iraq also provides an example of this phenomenon. The CIA had always been rather cool to the Bush White House's claims that Saddam Hussein was close to building a nuclear bomb. As late as February of 2002, CIA director George Tenet would go no further than to state, "We believe that Saddam never abandoned his nuclear weapons program." [35] When the CIA refused to give the administration the intelligence findings they wanted, the Bush administration created a new government office that would. The Policy Counterterrorism Group was set up in the Defense Department to act as a sort of alternative CIA. It reviewed raw intelligence files to pick out the information most supportive of the administration's pro-invasion policies. This information would in turn be funneled to another Defense Department office, the Office of Special Plans, to be used in analyses employed in briefing high administration officials, who would in turn repeat the dubious intelligence in speaking to Congress and the press.[36] And, of course, the administration in office can also distort the national debate by not compiling information that might be useful to its critics. A good example is the Bush administration's decision not to make determinations of the number of civilians killed or injured by American bombing of Iraq. And as we will also discuss in chapter 4, once combat has actually begun, the president has power to control access by the press to the war zone to report on combat operations.

All these factors magnify the power of presidential speech, but perhaps the most potent factor of all is the symbolic role the president plays in our political culture. The president's pronouncements on issues involving national security possess an authority no other speaker can approach. We all give special weight to the views of authority figures, and in the realm of foreign affairs, the president is the authority figure without peer. In times of peril like the aftermath of 9/11, he is the father figure we look to to protect us from harm. And in times of crisis we desire national unity, and the president is the symbolic representative of that unity, a fact that magnifies the power of presidential speech. Unfortunately, this yearning for unity often interferes with the democratic debate that actually better protects us from our enemies.

While the president also has great power to communicate on domestic issues, there are important differences between the president's power in the domestic and in the national security arenas. The relevant facts on domestic issues—like the future of Social Security—are available to all speakers; the psychological drive for unity is less pressing in the domestic arena, and on domestic issues the president is seen more as a leader of his political party than as leader of the nation. Even on domestic issues, he is the single most influential speaker, but he cannot overwhelm other voices. For instance, after his reelection in 2004, President Bush made a well-orchestrated attempt to persuade the American people that there was a need for a dramatic reshaping of the Social Security system. He was successful in getting his message across, but his critics were able to respond effectively. They had the same access to facts, were dealing with an issue on which most voters felt they were competent to judge, and did not have to face the president's special preeminence in the area of national security. President Bush was seen as a conservative politician instead of as our nation's leader. The president's arguments on Social Security were put to the test in a way that never materialized at the outset of the War on Terror.

There are limits to the power of presidential rhetoric. Not only does it not impact domestic issues in the same way as it does issues involving national security, but the power of presidential speech on national security issues eventually wanes when it is contradicted by publicly available facts. For instance, President Johnson's war policy was undermined by the inability of America and South Vietnam to prevail militarily in Vietnam just as President Bush's persuasiveness diminished as the insurgency in Iraq grew. But we should not take too much comfort from this fact. While it is true that presidential speech is less a danger on domestic issues, the resolution of national security issues necessarily impacts domestic issues by claiming the lion's share of both the political system's attention and the nation's financial resources. And while it is also true that a president's ability to dominate the national security debate diminishes in the face of evidence that his policy is failing, we can never return to the situation before he spoke. As the invasion of Iraq has demonstrated, presidential speech has consequences that are not reversed by proving him wrong at a later date.

Is It Constitutional?

I would like to return the question with which we began the book. A student or friend asks the seemingly simple question whether or not a certain act by the president is "constitutional." He or she asks whether President Bush's use of presidential speech to sell the invasion of Iraq violates the Constitution. A constitutional expert would be tempted to dismiss the question as hopelessly naïve. First, there is the problem of who would have standing to raise the issue in court. American courts require that a plaintiff show concrete injury before they will hear a lawsuit, but who can show such an injury caused by the president speaking his mind. Even if injury were shown, it is clear that the president has a right to speak both under his Article II powers and also as a citizen. Finally, there is no constitutional text or Supreme Court case even hinting at limits on the president's exercise of presidential speech. But I think the expert would be well advised to resist the temptation to dismiss such a question because in essence it frames what might be the most crucial constitutional issue of our era: Does the president's ability to manufacture consent on national security issues erode the democratic basis of the American Constitution?

It is remarkable that the issues of governmental speech in general and presidential speech on national security affairs in particular have had so little attention from courts and constitutional scholars. The Supreme Court has never spoken on the issue of presidential speech, and when faced with cases involving government speech has generally supported the government's right to speak its mind.[37] Constitutional scholars have also ignored the impact of presidential speech on democratic debate and have been more attentive to the general danger that government propaganda constitutes for democracy. For instance, Thomas Emerson clearly noted the danger of government speech in his important First Amendment treatise: "[I]t is very easy to visualize situations in which the government's voice may overwhelm and displace all others and thus distort the system of free expression."[38] Steven Shiffrin came to a similar conclusion in his highly regarded article on government speech: "[G]overnment can 'add its own voice to the many it must tolerate, provided it does not drown out private conversation.'"[39] And Mark Yudof's excellent book on government speech also discussed the threat that such speech presents to democratic government. "[I]f the government dominates the flow of ideas and information, the ideal of the self-controlled citizen, making informed choices about his government, is destroyed."[40] Yudof also argued that the

First Amendment should "prevent the distortion of the judgment of the people by government expression or secrecy."[41] While these scholars' conclusion that government speech should not "overwhelm" or "drown out" or "dominate" public debate describes the problem, none of them is very helpful with regard to practical solutions to the danger of presidential speech in the national security context. One reason for scholars' silence on this issue is that presidential speech seldom figures as an issue in court cases, the focus of most scholarly inquiry. We need a systemic perspective on how speech operates that recognizes that sometimes the Congress rather than the courts must play the leading role.

One of the fundamental principles of American First Amendment jurisprudence is found in Justice Louis Brandeis's statement in *Whitney v. California* that in a democracy the preferred "remedy to be applied is more speech, not enforced silence."[42] The preferred method is not to silence the president but to give competing voices a better chance to be heard. One such voice is the press; chapter 4 will discuss how the press can better perform its role of informing the people. Chapter 5 will show how added protection for the free speech activities of citizens' groups can also improve debate on national security issues. And chapter 6 argues that we must limit the president's ability to act first and debate later since such independent presidential actions render later debate impotent.

Another effective way to counter the dominance of presidential speech is to insist that the president speak more. Now we mostly hear presidents only when they give scripted messages in carefully chosen contexts. We may see the president address a wildly supportive audience against a background that emphasizes the majesty of his office. Sometimes we also hear presidents answering questions at press conferences, but press conferences take place only when the president chooses and the ground rules permit him to pick the questioners and give nonresponsive answers when he so chooses. In addition to these friendly speech events, we should also add a public forum in which members of Congress can regularly ask him the hard questions that a British prime minister regularly answers in the House of Commons. Congress should also call the president to testify before relevant committees, and to testify under oath when appropriate. The Congress is the president's partner in national security measures and should act and expect to be treated as such. Of course, some information must be kept secret from Congress and the public, but, as we will discuss in chapter 4, it is the role of courts, not the president, to be the final arbiter of what information should remain secret. And Congress can also require the executive branch to compile and publish more information necessary to national security debates, like the number of civilian casualties caused by military operations.

A Disinformation Felony

While I fully endorse Justice Brandeis's "more speech" philosophy of the First Amendment, I also believe that there is one area where the strategy of supporting more speech is inadequate: when presidents and their surrogates make knowing or recklessly false statements of fact on material national security issues. Often there is no effective method for critics to point out the lie, even if they have access to the true information, which they usually do not. We reviewed in chapter 1 examples of such intentional or reckless false statements on national security affairs made by presidents. For instance, President Eisenhower lied to the American people about the U2 plane's violation of Soviet air space, and President Reagan lied about the Iran/Contra weapons-for-hostages swap. And we know now that the alleged unprovoked attack on American ships in the Gulf of Tonkin by North Vietnamese gunboats that President Johnson used to persuade Congress to pass the Gulf of Tonkin Resolution probably never took place, a fact that Johnson was most likely aware of.

The most obvious example of such a statement in the invasion of Iraq occurred during President Bush's 2003 State of the Union address to Congress. President Bush made the following statement: "The British Government has learned that Saddam Hussein recently sought significant quantities of uranium from Africa." Evidence of Saddam's attempt to purchase a necessary ingredient in a nuclear device fit nicely in the Bush administration's case for war. Unfortunately, the story had already been tabbed as false by the CIA, which had concluded that earlier reports about Saddam's attempts to purchase "yellowcake" uranium in Niger were forgeries. In fact, the CIA had insisted that the allegation be removed from the pro-war speech Bush had made in Cincinnati a few months earlier. Suddenly the statement reappeared in President Bush's State of the Union address. The falsity of the statement was made public in an op-ed piece in the *New York Times* by former ambassador Joseph Wilson, who in 2002 had been sent to Niger by the CIA to determine the accuracy of such claims and had found them to be fabrications. Wilson charged that Bush had twisted facts to exaggerate the Iraqi threat.[43] Under fire, the Bush administration eventually admitted the error, responsibility for which was assumed by presidential aide Stephen Hadley. Hadley's punishment was to later be appointed President Bush's national security advisor. Certainly the statement did not place itself in the speech; someone added it. Even its studied phrasing (did Bush attribute the claim to the British government because he knew that the CIA believed the claim to be patently false?) suggests that it was a carefully considered addition. And it is highly unlikely that President Bush, in reviewing the text, was not aware of the CIA's earlier rejection of the Niger yellowcake story. One cannot help but suspect that President Bush was less concerned with the truth or falsity of the claim than with the fact that it appeared to provide the much-sought-after "smoking gun" of Saddam's intent to produce nuclear weapons.[44]

It is testimony to the special status of the presidency that we are so shocked that presidents would mislead us. No one believes that politicians as a class are above shading the truth, and presidents are politicians. Falsehoods are part of the game. Richard Nixon is reported to have once said, "If you can't lie, you'll never go anywhere."[45] I think that an exchange between Secretary of State Colin Powell and vice-presidential aide Scooter Libby, related in Ron Suskind's book *The One Percent Doctrine*,[46] gives us a sense of how public officials sometimes view the boundaries between truth and falsehood on statements relative to national security. Powell had used information provided by Libby in his controversial presentation to the United Nations Security Council just before the invasion of Iraq. In that presentation, Powell made the case that Saddam Hussein was engaged in producing nuclear weapons. Later, when no weapons were discovered, critics started questioning the factual basis of Powell's arguments. Powell in turn accused Libby of providing Powell with false information. Libby not only rejected the charge but reconfigured the issue, arguing that Powell's presentation was not meant to be a balanced disquisition on the facts but rather "an argument that a lawyer might make in a courtroom."[47] To use a phrase coined by comedian Stephen Colbert, it no longer appears necessary for government statements to be true so long as they possess the quality of "truthiness"—they sound like they are true and actually might be true.

I am willing to concede that presidents and other highly placed officials usually only make false statements in a good-faith belief that the falsehood is justified by larger national security interests. But their good faith does not change the fact that such intentional or reckless false statements distort public debate on national security issues. They corrupt the free speech system. And we also must keep in mind that it is easy for presidents and other high officials to experience confusion as to when a falsehood is really necessary and when it is merely in the speaker's short-term political interests. And if we accept the fact that presidents make knowing or recklessly false statements, we condone the practice.

Instead, Congress should make it a felony for the president, the vice-president, and cabinet-level officials to make public false statements on material national security issues with knowledge or reckless disregard of their falsity. Such a statute would clearly be politically controversial and would be challenged on the constitutional grounds that it would violate the separation of powers and the First Amendment. Both challenges would require us to consider to what extent falsehoods are necessary to effective democratic government. Courts have disagreed about the constitutionality of state statutes punishing knowing or recklessly false statement by candidates in political campaigns.[48] To answer the question whether a congressional statute punishing knowing or reckless falsehoods by high officials about national security issues would be constitutionally permissible, we have to consider both the value of the speech prohibited and the governmental interests that justify the ban. False statements in themselves have little constitutional value. The Supreme Court has consistently upheld the right of states to punish calculated lies.[49] But we have to face up to the fact that prohibitions on false speech may have the effect of deterring true speech. This is the "chilling effect" the Supreme Court spoke about in its opinion in *New York Times v. Sullivan* when discussing whether the First Amendment prohibited punishing the press for publishing libelous falsehoods without knowledge of their falsity.[50] The Supreme Court in that case resolved this dilemma in the libel context by removing free speech protection from only some false statements, those "made with 'actual malice'—this is knowledge that it was false or with reckless disregard whether it was false or not."[51] If plaintiff could show that the newspaper knew its statements to be false or showed reckless disregard as to whether they were true or false, a libel judgment was permissible. The court reasoned that while we cannot ask a newspaper to guarantee that a falsehood never appears in its pages, we can ask them to take reasonable steps to weed out errors. We can expect the same of the president and other high-level executive branch officials

The "actual malice" standard has worked well in the area of libel awards for almost half a century. There is no reason why it would not work just as well with regard to high-level statements by executive branch officials on national security issues since these officials, like newspapers, have large staffs to check out the accuracy of factual statements. It is important that the statute be clear that it is only the false statements of fact that are covered by the statute, not opinions that can't be shown to be true or false.[52] Added protections would be provided by the prosecution's need to prove the felony beyond a reasonable doubt, as well as by independent appellate review of any conviction. The statute could further reduce the chilling effect on presidential speech by providing a provision excluding from coverage false statements that are quickly corrected.

The primary rationale for criminalizing knowing or reckless falsehoods about national security issues is their distorting effect on democratic debate. The Supreme Court itself has endorsed this "distortion" rationale in upholding congressional statutes limiting campaign contributions.[53] The same reasoning would apply to a congressional disinformation statute. And we should also realize, as in the campaign finance context, that free speech values support the statute as well as the president's right to unregulated speech. Supreme Court justice Stephen Breyer has argued that statutes limiting campaign contributions have a greater claim to constitutional validity because their goal is to "help to further the kind of open political discussion that the First Amendment seeks to encourage. . . ."[54] The national security disinformation legislation has this same prospeech goal.

I doubt there would be many, if any, prosecutions under such a statute since we cannot expect that the attorney general who serves at the president's sufferance will show much enthusiasm for prosecuting the president or his surrogates. But the very existence of the statute would give presidents and their aides reason to be more careful in their choice of words and to think twice about making statements that they know may not be true. And it would also have political effects since violation of such a statute would clearly constitute a "high crime or misdemeanor" and therefore provide grounds for impeachment.

A disinformation statute might to some degree transform the rough-and-tumble style of political speech that Americans relish. We usually prefer to allow the rhetorical chips to fall where they may and only allow the audience to determine issues of truth and falsity. But some limitation on presidential speech may be a necessary exception to this general rule. The president's unrivaled access to the media, when combined with the public's lack of access to the true facts underlying his statements on national security, may require that we demand that he be careful in making statements of fact about national security.

The Rise and Fall of
the First Amendment

*We consider this case against the background of a profound
national commitment to the principle that debate on public issues should be uninhibited, robust, and wide-open. . . .*
— Justice William Brennan

I have argued in the first two chapters that the National Security Presidency and the singular powers of presidential speech threaten to corrupt our debate on national security issues. I believe that the necessary
constitutional response to this danger is an expansive interpretation of the
First Amendment that ensures that opposing voices will be heard. In the
1960s, in a series of free speech cases involving civil rights, the Supreme
Court gave us a good start towards such an interpretation, and this chapter
begins by describing those cases. Readers may wonder why I choose to discuss cases concerning a domestic issue like civil rights that took place fifty
years ago. Not only are the free speech cases of the sixties still relevant today
but also recognition of the way these Supreme Court decisions affected the
outcome of the civil rights struggle illustrates the fact that Supreme Court
First Amendment rulings have substantial political effects. And these cases
also remind us of how citizens with little financial or electoral clout can
play a meaningful role in the decisions that affect their lives.

A Short History of the First Amendment

We usually think of the First Amendment as a reassuring symbol of our
long-standing national commitment to individual expression and robust

political debate. Actually, the history of the First Amendment is much more complex, and the prominent role it plays in American political life of a much more recent origin, than usually supposed. The Bill of Rights was tacked on to the original text of the Constitution in 1791 as part of a political deal to attract sufficient votes to secure that document's ratification. In substance, the Bill of Rights mostly concerns criminal-procedure rights like the ban on unreasonable searches and seizures, the right to a jury trial, and the right against self-incrimination. The major exception is the First Amendment. Its text not only addresses the thorny issue of religion but also proudly promises that Congress shall not "abridge" the rights of free speech, free press, peaceful assembly, and petition for the redress of grievances.[1] There was disagreement about the amendment's meaning from the very beginning. For instance, when Congress passed the Sedition Act of 1798 to punish, among other things, statements that brought the president into "contempt or disrepute," there were vociferous disputes about whether such "seditious" statements were protected by the First Amendment, even though many of the senators and congressmen who passed the amendment were still in office.

This lack of clarity, combined with the fact that the amendment only applied to federal legislation at a time when the vast majority of laws were passed by the individual states, resulted in the First Amendment playing a very small role in American politics during the nineteenth and early twentieth centuries. As late as 1907, the Supreme Court in *Patterson v. Colorado*[2] cavalierly rejected a free speech defense to a state court contempt judgment without even conceding that the First Amendment applied to state statutes.

The Holmes-Brandeis Dissents

The First Amendment was resurrected by means of a series of brilliant dissents by Justices Oliver Wendell Holmes and Louis Brandeis in the 1920s in cases involving laws punishing antiwar dissent during World War I. Their first famous dissent was in *Abrams v. United States.*[3] *Abrams* involved the conviction of a group of Socialists for distributing pamphlets at a munitions factory that urged the workers not to produce arms the protestors thought the U.S. government would use against the new Bolshevik government in Russia. The defendants had been convicted under a federal statute that made it a crime to incite work stoppages of armaments necessary for the war effort. On First Amendment issues, the Supreme Court at that time was employing what experts call the "bad tendency" test—any speech could be punished if its natural consequence was to bring about the mischief that the statute prohibited.[4] If the natural tendency of distributing pamphlets urging workers not to make armaments was to lower worker productivity and therefore interfere with the war effort, the distribution of the pamphlets was not protected by the First Amendment. The government need not prove that the workers were persuaded by the pamphlets or that worker productivity actually was lowered or that war production decreased; it need only show that the speech had taken place.

Justice Holmes, in a dissent joined by Justice Brandeis, ignored the "bad tendency" test and instead argued that the First Amendment required that punishing speech should always be the last resort, available only to counteract some immediate serious danger or, as he phrased it, "a clear and present danger." Since there was no evidence to support the proposition that the pamphlets posed a clear and present danger to the war effort, the dissent concluded that the protesters were protected by the First Amendment. The *Abrams* dissent was followed by a series of other cases in which Holmes and Brandeis filed other dissents, further articulating the "clear and present danger" test. They insisted that the danger be both serious and imminent and that the judge must decide whether these constitutional requirements were present.

The Holmes-Brandeis dissents are now recognized as classic statements of American First Amendment jurisprudence. What was not recognized at the time was that while the two justices agreed on the "clear and present danger" rule, they arrived at it from different philosophical paths.[5] Holmes, the patrician skeptic, had little faith in democracy, which he saw as government by the ill-informed masses. His dissent in *Abrams* never mentions democracy. Instead, it relied on the metaphor of a marketplace of ideas—"the best test of truth is the power of the thought to get itself accepted in the competition of the market."[6] Holmes warned against government interference with the marketplace of ideas because, like an economic market, the intellectual market works better without government interference.

Louis Brandeis came to the Court after a brilliant career as a practitioner, both of corporate law and of what we now would call public interest law. Brandeis was a strong advocate for democratic government, as his classic concurrence in *Whitney v. California*[7] makes clear. Brandeis's opinion never mentions Holmes's marketplace of ideas; instead, he speaks of how important citizen participation is to democratic government: "the greatest menace to freedom is an inert people, [and] public discussion is a political duty."[8] Brandeis's concurrence is the first modern statement of the democratic self-government principle, the constitutional vision that I believe should guide First Amendment doctrine today. Brandeis made clear that the First Amendment should be more concerned with the ability of citizens to have their voices heard than with abstract concepts like the marketplace of ideas.

The Holmes-Brandeis position on freedom of speech eventually achieved majority status. In 1931 in *Near v. Minnesota,*[9] the Supreme Court for the first time expressly struck down a state statute as a violation of the First Amendment as incorporated in the Fourteenth Amendment's Due Process Clause. And the Court issued other decisions in the 1930s and 1940s consistent with the self-government principle. In the 1937 case of *DeJonge v. Oregon,*[10] the Court declared that the "right of peaceful assembly is a right just as important as those of free speech and a free press." So thereafter, the Court in *Hague v. CIO*[11] held for the first time that the First Amendment required that streets and parks be open to political demonstrations.

The McCarthy Era

But this movement towards a more speech-friendly political culture was suddenly reversed in the late 1940s and early 1950s by a national hysteria caused by charges that Soviet spies had infiltrated the highest levels of American government.[12] In response, government programs were launched at the national and state level to punish "disloyal" speech. Turning its back on the spirit of the Holmes-Brandeis dissents and the pro–free speech rulings of the thirties and forties, the Supreme Court began to approve speech-repressive statutes as consistent with the First Amendment.

The most famous case was *Dennis v. United States.*[13] It involved the conviction of the leaders of the Communist Party under a federal statute banning advocacy of the forcible overthrow of the government. The Communist Party played a dual role in American life during the thirties and forties; it was both a spy organization and a mass-based political party. The spy organization was made up of a small number of operatives who tried, sometimes successfully, to infiltrate the federal government. The mass political party publicized left-wing issues like the failures of capitalism and the evils of segregation in the South. The political party attained a membership perhaps as high as one hundred thousand people in the later thirties and early forties before declining as a political force. During the 1950s the FBI infiltrated the party. A commonly told joke claimed that by the mid-1950s most of the party's dues-paying members were FBI agents.

But the advent of the Cold War and the discovery that a few Soviet spies had been members of the party led demagogues like Senator Joseph McCarthy to mount a campaign to rid American government of anyone with any left-wing connections in their past. Advocacy of Communist ideology was now a federal crime, and past membership in the Communist Party or connections with any group associated with the party were often the causes for loss of employment as well as social disgrace. Federal and state commissions were created to root out "disloyal" employees, and those who wished to clear their names of disloyalty were encouraged to implicate others to demonstrate their own loyalty. Democratic liberals who had flirted with left-wing issues during the Depression were now presumptively disloyal. Even attending a meeting of a left-wing organization or signing a petition later linked to a left-wing organization could suddenly end a successful professional career.[14]

The defendants in the *Dennis* case were prosecuted under a statute that made advocacy of the overthrow of the American government by violence a federal felony. The Communist leaders accused of this crime had not in fact taken any concrete steps to bring about the violent overthrow of the government, but they had taught that someday the masses would rise up to throw off the shackles of capitalism. A majority of the Supreme Court thought this was sufficient evidence to uphold their convictions for conspiracy to advocate the violent overthrow of the government. In reaching this conclusion, so alien to the free speech philosophy of the Holmes-Brandeis dissents, Chief Justice Vinson's opinion used the term "clear and present danger" but transformed its meaning by holding that the more serious the danger, the less imminent the threat need be. He reasoned that although any actual violent revolution was far off, the overthrow of democratic government was such a serious evil that its advocacy could be punished long before the danger became imminent. And in determining the severity of the future threat, the Court believed that judges should be deferential to the judgment of elected officials. This sounded much more like the "bad tendency" approach to free speech that Holmes and Brandeis had rejected than the "clear and present danger" test that insisted on both imminent danger and judicial independence. We see in the *Dennis* majority opinion a deference to government claims about national security that would mark judicial opinions after 9/11.

The Civil Rights Movement

It is against this dark constitutional backdrop that the modern civil rights movement began its attempt to end segregation in the South.[15] The Supreme Court's decision in *Brown v. Bd. of Education*[16] had declared that state-mandated segregation violated the Fourteenth Amendment's Equal Protection Clause, but this had little concrete effect on the lives of African-Americans in the South. We tend to identify the civil rights movement with the heroism of Martin Luther King Jr. King's eloquence was extremely important, but Dr. King would be the first to insist that we recognize the civil rights movement as a multifaceted effort in which a large variety of different citizens' groups played essential roles; different groups used different tactics. The National Association for the Advancement of Colored People's (NAACP) preferred tool was litigation while King's Southern Christian Leadership Conference (SLC) engaged in boycotts and mass marches.

All civil rights groups were threatened by a phalanx of southern laws designed to silence opponents of segregation. We sometimes assume that humans are all civil libertarians at heart, enthusiastically waiting to hear viewpoints that challenge our deeply held beliefs. History shows this to be a false view. As Justice Holmes said in the *Abrams* case, "Persecution for the expression of opinion seems to me perfectly logical. If you have no doubt about your premises or your power and want a certain result with all your heart you naturally express your wishes in law and sweep away all opposition."[17]

The truth is that we need the First Amendment *because* we are instinctively hostile to opposing ideas and our natural instinct is to squash them. The response of southern political leaders to the civil rights movement illustrates this psychological truth. They believed with all their hearts in the legitimacy of segregation and were willing to use the law to sweep away all opposition to the racial status quo. The fact that segregation was based on a belief in the supremacy of the white race made it no less attractive to the vast majority of white southerners.

The southern response to the Supreme Court's ruling in *Brown* was a categorical rejection of the legitimacy of the ruling and the adoption of a strategy of what Southern leaders themselves termed "massive resistance" to any change in the racial status quo. One of the primary political strategies of "massive resistance" was the passage and enforcement of laws designed to nullify the efforts of civil rights advocates. Throughout American history, officials who wished to repress a political message usually made dissemination of the message a crime. We earlier noted that the infamous Sedition Act of 1798 made it a crime to criticize government officials. The federal government took the same approach during World War I in criminalizing the speech of dissenters like the pamphleteers in *Abrams*. It speaks to the growing American consensus on the importance of free speech that such crude forms of censorship were not attempted during the civil rights era. But that does not mean that the desire to silence dissent disappeared; it just took more sophisticated forms.

Southern leaders originally attributed their racial troubles to the activities of the NAACP and therefore put a lot of effort into defeating that organization.[18] Some states, like Alabama and Louisiana, tried to stop all activities of the NAACP within their borders. In fact, the NAACP was effectively closed down in Alabama during the early years of the civil rights movement. Others, like Virginia, tried to stymie NAACP litigation efforts by making it a crime to solicit plaintiffs for civil rights suits. Still other states made membership in the NAACP a cause for the loss of government employment, a serious threat since a large percentage of NAACP members were public school teachers. And since the state could not terminate teachers for belonging to the NAACP unless it knew which teachers were indeed members, states also passed laws requiring teachers to divulge their organizational memberships.

But the South's targets extended well beyond the NAACP. The goal was to stifle any public expression of dissent on the issue of segregation. Southern white leaders wanted to intimidate anyone who might even think of opposing segregation. Economic retaliation was one important tool in this attempt to (in the words of one candid segregationist) "make it difficult, if not impossible, for any Negro who advocates desegregation to find or hold a job, get credit, or renew a mortgage."[19] Here legislative investigations of civil right groups were often more effective than criminal prosecutions since the investigations publicized the names of individual civil rights activists, making them easy targets for private economic retaliation.

Demonstrations and protests against segregation were special targets of repression. Southern officials showed great legal resourcefulness in the techniques they employed to silence civil rights advocates. One target was the civil rights demonstrations that attracted so much press coverage. Laws requiring a permit to march were quite useful to the segregationist cause. If a permit application for a demonstration were filed, a ruling on it could be delayed until after the date of the proposed march. If the demonstrators marched without a permit, the march could be enjoined as in violation of the permit law itself. If a demonstration—like the "sit-ins" at segregated lunch counters—took place on private property, the protesters were prosecuted under trespass laws. If the demonstration took place on public property, they were prosecuted under "breach of peace" or "disorderly conduct" statutes. In addition, the leaders advocating the protests might be charged with inciting crime, and additional charges of "resisting arrest" could be tagged onto any arrests that took place. We will see in chapter 5 that government officials after 9/11 also devised new "legal" means to silence dissent.

The architects of massive resistance to integration also recognized the importance of the press. For the most part, the local white newspapers and radio and television stations were enthusiastic supporters of the segregationist cause; those who strayed from the segregationist line could usually be corrected by pressure from important advertisers. The northern press presented a different problem; the projection of negative images of southern racism had a dramatic effect in increasing northern support for the civil rights movement. Here southern officials felt that they could use defamation laws to deter northern newspapers from publishing negative stories about segregation. Small factual errors in negative press accounts in northern newspapers of civil rights controversies could be presented to all-white local juries as vicious assaults on the good names of southern officials with confidence that large damage awards would result.

And although our focus here is on "legal" techniques used to silence civil rights dissent, we should not forget that there was also a good deal of lawless violence aimed at civil rights activists during the 1960s. Perhaps the most notorious was the murder of three civil rights workers in Mississippi during the Freedom Summer of 1964. While southern authorities were eager to prosecute allegedly illegal conduct by civil rights activists, they were less eager to investigate and prosecute these violent crimes when they were committed by supporters of segregation against civil rights workers. Historian Norman Bartley accurately sums up the atmosphere of violence that permeated the South during that time when he says, "Throughout most of the South . . . a person who publicly deviated on social issues was fortunate if he was harassed only by threatening phone calls."[20]

The Warren Court's First Amendment

It is important to remember that the techniques that the South used to silence civil rights activists had good support in existing law; they involved either using statutes already on the books or writing new statutes that crafted well-established legal principles to fit the goal of resisting social change. Whether or not the southern attack on dissent would succeed depended on how the federal courts—especially the U.S. Supreme Court—responded to claims by civil rights activists that southern tactics violated the First Amendment. And the Supreme Court's recent narrow readings of the First Amendment in cases like *Dennis* gave the South reason for optimism.

But the Supreme Court changed both its membership and its direction. The makeup of the court was changed in the 1950s and 1960s by Presidents Eisenhower's, Kennedy's, and Johnson's use of the appointment power. Eisenhower appointed the liberal Republican governor of California as chief justice, reportedly as a reward for Earl Warren's support for Eisenhower at the Republican convention in 1952. Eisenhower also appointed William Brennan to the Court in 1956; here, too, politics played a role. Eisenhower felt it would help him in the 1956 presidential election to appoint a Democrat and a Roman Catholic to the Court. Brennan qualified on both counts. Both Warren and Brennan took a more activist stance in regard to individual rights issues like freedom of speech. They joined with two old liberal war horses from the New Deal era, Hugo Black and William O. Douglas, to form the nucleus of what would come to be known as the "Warren Court."

Harvard historian Morton Horwitz notes that all four justices shared "outsider" origins that made them suspicious of established power.[21] Hugo Black was born on a farm in poor, rural Alabama. Douglas was raised by his widowed mother in Washington State. Warren was the son of a Scandinavian immigrant who held a low-level job with the Southern Pacific railroad in California. Brennan's father, also an immigrant, worked as a metal polisher before rising to political importance in New Jersey. Having come from poor or working-class backgrounds, they knew that the legal status quo was not always fair.

One striking difference between their biographies and that of the conservative judges who make up the conservative majority on the Supreme Court today was their experience in politics. All four also had backgrounds in politics that permitted them to view with some skepticism government arguments that decisions protecting individual rights were incompatible with effective government. Black had been a powerful New Deal senator and Douglas had been the chairman of the Securities and Exchange Commission under Franklin Roosevelt. Earl Warren was a popular two-term California governor. While Brennan had no formal political experience, he was the son of a politician. Unlike contemporary conservative justices, who often move from elite law schools to prestigious clerkships to appointments to the federal bench early in their careers, the Warren Court justices were well acquainted with how government worked and less willing to uncritically defer to government explanations of why individual rights had to be sacrificed. This suspicion of established power, combined with confidence in their own political judgment, made them open to the constitutional arguments made by the civil rights advocates.

The appointment of Justice Brennan was important in many ways. First, he constituted a fourth vote for a strong First Amendment, only one away from a majority. Brennan also brought considerable interpersonal skills to a polarized court, keeping channels of communication open to moderate conservatives like John Harlan and Potter Stewart, two justices who often provided the crucial fifth vote for a free speech majority. Brennan also devised the doctrinal formula that would constitute the Warren Court's primary technique for free speech issues. While Douglas and Black had written strong free speech dissents during the McCarthy period, they both tended to talk of the First Amendment in absolutist terms. Brennan took a different rhetorical tack, one that constitutional historian Lucas Powe has aptly described as "the technique of approving ends, but finding fault with the means."[22] Unlike Black, Brennan never claimed that First Amendment protections were absolute, and he usually was willing to concede that the government had an important goal in mind when limiting speech. Instead, he questioned the means adopted to achieve that goal, arguing that more narrowly focused measures could achieve the government's goal with less deterrent effect on speech. This less absolutist approach made it much easier to attract the necessary fifth vote.

Arthur Goldberg's appointment in 1962 to replace the conservative Felix Frankfurter brought the fifth vote Warren, Brennan, Black, and Douglas needed. When Goldberg left the Court in 1965 to serve as Lyndon Johnson's ambassador to the United Nations, he was replaced by the equally liberal Abe Fortas. In 1967, former NAACP general counsel Thurgood Marshall's appointment provided a sixth pro–free speech vote, although this addition was neutralized in large part by Justice Black's growing conservatism on free speech issues in the late 1960s. Still, from 1962 until Warren's retirement in 1969, the Warren Court majority used its power to refashion American constitutional law on many issues, none more important than the First Amendment. A new official interpretation of the First Amendment emerged.

Opening the System to Change

The Warren Court handed down a large number of decisions interpreting provisions of the First Amendment. Even if we exclude the decisions interpreting the Free Exercise[23] and Establishment Clauses,[24] there are many important Warren Court First Amendment decisions—on issues like obscenity[25]—that do not relate directly to the topic of national security. This section will focus on a series of cases that I believe are especially relevant to discussion of security issues today.

Brandenburg v. Ohio[26] is such a case. In the excitement of a civil rights demonstration, there could be a thin line between the fiery denunciation of injustice and incitement to violence. Therefore, speakers were always vulnerable to criminal prosecution for words that mentioned the possibility of violence but were not intended to incite violent deeds. While Justices Holmes and Brandeis had taken the position that criminalizing advocacy of violence was only permissible when the government could show that the advocacy created a "clear and present danger" of being immediately acted upon, we saw that the 1951 *Dennis* decision had watered that formula down to allow punishment of advocacy of violence that might take place in the distant future.

In *Brandenburg,* the Warren Court reinstated and even expanded the Holmes-Brandeis protections. *Brandenburg* involved what might be called a reverse civil rights fact pattern. A Ku Klux Klan leader was prosecuted under an Ohio statute forbidding advocacy of violence. He had spoken at a Klan meeting and said, among other things, that "if our President, our Congress, our Supreme Court, continue to suppress the white, Caucasian race, it's possible that there might have to be some revengeance [sic] taken."[27] Justice Brennan's opinion not only reversed the conviction but also set out a new standard states had to meet for punishing advocacy of illegal political action. Now states could not "forbid or proscribe advocacy of the use of force or of law violation except where such advocacy is directed to inciting or producing imminent lawless action and is likely to incite or produce such action."[28] This formulation not only reestablished the "imminence" requirement central to the Holmes-Brandeis approach but also improved upon it by making clear that advocacy of immediate action was not enough; the state had to prove that the advocacy was likely to be acted upon. Judicial focus was returned to the illegal conduct caused, not the advocacy itself.[29]

NAACP v. Alabama[30] is a good example of how the Warren Court created new First Amendment structural rights. In this case they fashioned a right of internal privacy for citizens' groups. At the beginning of the civil rights struggle southern officials blamed the NAACP for most of their troubles and hoped that the group could be neutralized by economic pressure applied to its individual members. In the lawsuit arising out of Alabama's attempt to enjoin the NAACP from operating in the state, Alabama demanded that the NAACP provide the names of its members in the state, an act that would make the members vulnerable to harassment and discourage membership. The NAACP refused, but its position initially appeared weak from a First Amendment perspective since Alabama was not prohibiting it from speaking but only asking for information arguably relevant to a lawsuit. But the Court's opinion in *NAACP v. Alabama* cured this weakness by connecting the right of group association to free speech, thereby creating an independent right of political association. The Court reasoned that the privacy of the internal workings of an association, like membership lists, had to be protected because "[e]ffective advocacy of both public and private points of view, particularly controversial ones, is undeniably enhanced by group association. . . ."[31] Here the Court recognized and supported the crucial role that citizens' groups play in modern democratic debate. Groups, not lone individuals, are the prime movers in campaigns for political change. The group has not only the ability to nurture the growth of unconventional ideas but also the organizational capacity to effectively publicize them. In modern mass democracies, the lonely pamphleteer is doomed to irrelevance; only well-organized groups can effect political change. And the Court's holding in

NAACP v. Alabama recognized the undisputed fact that membership in activist groups like the NAACP would plummet if they were forced to disclose the names of their members to the government.

Brandenburg protected incendiary speech; *NAACP v. Alabama* protected the privacy of activist groups like the NAACP. A third line of cases opened up the streets and parks to the large public demonstrations so crucial to the success of the civil rights movement. One way groups publicize their proposals for change is through protests that will attract press attention. The civil rights movement's primary tool for publicizing its anti-segregation message was the peaceful mass march. We noted earlier that southern officials often responded by arresting protesters for violation of breach-of-the-peace laws. In the 1963 case of *Edwards v. South Carolina*,[32] a group of African-American students had peacefully marched on the grounds of the South Carolina state house to deliver to the legislature a petition against unfair treatment of Negroes. When a white crowd gathered, the police asked the protesters to disperse and then arrested them for breach of the peace when they refused. The protesters claimed that the subsequent convictions violated their rights of free speech, free assembly, and freedom to petition for redress of grievances, all rights mentioned in the text of the First Amendment. The Supreme Court reversed the convictions because the protesters had engaged in "an exercise of these basic constitutional rights in the most pristine and classic form."[33] This made clear that the First Amendment protection went beyond speech to include conduct like marching. While the right to march was not absolute, it could be regulated by the state only by means of neutrally applied laws, like those relating to traffic control, that were narrowly drawn to allow as much speech as practicable. In *Brown v. Louisiana*,[34] the Court even extended the First Amendment "public forum" beyond traditional protest sites like streets and parks to other government property. In *Brown*, five young African-Americans stood silently in a branch library to protest its segregated lending policies. The Court held that the demonstration was protected by the First Amendment so long as it did not disrupt the library's primary function as a quiet place for reading and study.

And the Warren Court also interpreted the First Amendment as protecting the press's right to inform the public on important issues like civil rights. Protest is only effective if it is reported. Southern leaders hoped that aggressive use of libel laws would help silence the northern press, which had been so active in publicizing the civil rights message. The key here was to find some factual error in an article mentioning a public official; the error could then be used by the official as the basis for a defamation action that would result in a large award of damages by an all-white southern jury. The perfect vehicle for trying out this strategy appeared when a fund-raising appeal by Martin Luther King Jr.'s Southern Christian Leadership Council (SCLC) appeared in the *New York Times*. The paid advertisement described events that took place at Alabama State University in Montgomery after student protests there had provoked police action. The ad gave a mostly accurate account of what had transpired but contained some minor factual errors. For instance, it said that the authorities had padlocked the school cafeteria when all they had done was to refuse admittance to students who had refused to register for classes. Also, the ad said that police had "ringed" the campus while in fact the police had gathered on only one side of the campus. But under Alabama law these factual errors were libel—and not only were they libelous, but since they referred to elected officials in performance of their official duties, they permitted an Alabama jury to award not only actual but also "presumed" damages.

The first plaintiff was Montgomery police commissioner L. B. Sullivan, who sued for five hundred thousand dollars in damages, at the time an extraordinary amount of money. Sullivan soon was followed by four other plaintiffs with similar complaints. The potential consequences were very serious for the *New York Times*, a newspaper already on shaky financial footing. Officials at the *Times* were so upset by the suit that they ordered their reporters to stay out of Alabama until the issue was resolved. If successful, the Sullivan suit would have substantially curtailed, if not silenced, northern press coverage of the civil rights movement.

Worse yet, Sullivan had a very solid case under state defamation law, and the Supreme Court had in earlier cases expressly excluded libel from the protection of the First Amendment.[35] The Court's landmark opinion in *New York Times v. Sullivan*[36] changed all this by protecting the important role the press plays in informing the public on political issues. Justice Brennan's opinion echoed Brandeis's emphasis on the importance of democratic debate:

> We consider this case against the background of a profound national commitment to the principle that debate on public issues should be uninhibited, robust, and widespread, and it may well include vehement, caustic, and sometimes unpleasantly sharp attacks on government and public officials.[37]

From this broad major premise Brennan concluded that good faith statements about public officials, even if false, received a qualified First Amendment immunity from libel liability; false statements now were only punishable if made with knowledge of the falsity or reckless disregard of whether or not the statement was false. The Court soon extended the Sullivan rule beyond public officials like Sullivan. In *Associated Press v. Walker*[38] the Court held that a segregationist agitator had to meet the heavy *New York Times v. Sullivan* burden in his suit for libel. The press was now free to report on public controversies without fear of crippling damage awards. The *New York Times* decision paid large democratic dividends in the form of the press's reporting on civil rights, the war in Vietnam, and, later, the Watergate scandal

Activists opposing government policy were then (as they are now) vulnerable to prosecution under loosely phrased statutes that could be used to deter expression of political dissent. To respond to this evil, the Court employed the doctrine of unconstitutional overbreadth. Perhaps no other doctrinal innovation better symbolizes the Warren Court's structural approach to First Amendment issues. Overbreadth is premised on the belief that the very existence of a statute that authorizes prosecution of clearly protected free speech activity creates an improper disincentive (or "chill") on speech even before the law is enforced. In *Dombrowski v. Pfister*[39] the Court struck down a Louisiana statute with extremely broad language that would have authorized prosecution of clearly protected First Amendment activity even though a prosecution was never initiated. The overbreadth doctrine is a reminder to legislatures that they should draft their statutes as narrowly as possible to avoid unnecessary chilling of political dissent.

I wish to emphasize how these individual doctrines reinforced one another, creating a synergy that magnified their individual effect. And just as important as the scope of the activities protected was the methodology the Court employed in individual cases. Critics often suggest that we have to choose between free speech and effective government, but the Warren Court created a flexible methodology that advanced free speech interests in concrete cases without denying the importance of other governmental goals. Free speech rights, like other constitutional rights, are not absolute; they must be harmonized with other important governmental goals like the prevention of violence or the preservation of national security. While not denying the importance of these governmental interests, the Warren Court did look carefully to ensure that free speech rights were not unnecessarily sacrificed. The Warren Court majority made no absolutist claims for free speech. Instead, the Court made clear that free speech interests sometimes had to yield to other compelling governmental goals, but insisted that the government choose the most speech-protective means available. In *Shelton v. Tucker*,[40] Arkansas officials had asked every public school teacher to list every organization he or she had belonged to in the past five years. It was common knowledge that the state intended to fire all the teachers who admitted membership in the NAACP. The Court's opinion conceded that Arkansas had good reason to look into the competency of its teachers and agreed that the way they used their time outside of class might be relevant to that inquiry. But it also questioned the legislative means used to achieve the goal. Asking teachers to list every organization was too broad an inquiry, one that would chill their right to join groups like the NAACP that they knew their employers did not like. Therefore, the Court insisted that the "breadth of the legislative infringement must be viewed in light of less drastic means for achieving the same basic purpose."[41] The Court suggested that Arkansas could achieve its goal with less impact on the right of association if it inquired into the amount of time teachers spent on outside activities rather than the names of the organizations they joined. This way the state could achieve its goal of ensuring that teachers had time to do their job without interfering with their First Amendment rights. This demand for use of the least restrictive alternative forced legislatures to include concern for free speech rights in their legislative plans.

These cases, and other like them, had political impact. The First Amendment–protected activities of the civil rights groups and the press culminated in the passing of two landmark civil rights statutes, the Civil Rights Act of 1964 and the Voting Rights Act of 1965. But we must recognize that it was not protest alone that resulted in reform. The civil rights groups were successful in persuading the Democratic Party to make civil rights a major part of their legislative program, but it was President Johnson's skillful use of the power of presidential speech that brought about the passage of the civil rights legislation.

The Vietnam War

The Warren Court applied and expanded the free speech principles developed in the civil rights cases to new issues arising from the Vietnam War. Some might question whether antiwar voices deserve the same protection as civil rights advocates. African-Americans had a special knowledge of the evils of segregation that antiwar protesters could not claim with respect to national security. One might say that every citizen cannot be his or her own secretary of state. But this objection misunderstands the reason for freedom of speech in a democracy. Citizens have a right to speak not because they are experts but because they have a right to a voice in decisions that affect their lives. And we should also remember that antiwar protesters added important insights to the Vietnam debate that government experts missed. While the experts were talking about the needs of geopolitics, antiwar demonstrators condemned the war as a violation of America's democratic ideals, a postcolonial war waged on a nonwhite people with an army of draftees disproportionately composed of nonwhite American soldiers.

The Vietnam War, like most wars, was popular at the beginning.[42] Almost 70 percent of Americans polled supported President Johnson's decision to bomb North Vietnam in the spring of 1965. But some citizens' groups, already active on issues like civil rights and nuclear disarmament, did not share the majority's visceral patriotic response to the war. These groups saw American involvement not only as diverting attention from more important issues like civil rights but also as inconsistent with America's democratic ideals. Groups like Students for a Democratic Society (SDS), Women's Strike for Peace, and Committee for a Sane Nuclear Policy (SANE) organized protests against the growing American involvement. For instance, as early as April 1965, SDS brought twenty thousand antiwar protesters to Washington. It was a sign of things to come.

Over the next three years, the antiwar movement gained momentum, improvising new forms of political protest as it grew in strength. In the spring of 1965, antiwar protesters employed a deliberative mode by holding "teach-ins" at elite universities like the University of Michigan and the University of California at Berkeley. Soon these were followed by large, peaceful marches against the war. In the fall of 1965, one hundred thousand protesters marched in cities all over the United States. The marches continued to grow as opposition to the war expanded. In the spring of 1967, three hundred thousand people attended a demonstration against the war in New York City's Central Park.

But when these protests failed to change Johnson administration policy, more aggressive tactics were employed. Some groups moved from education and protest to civil disobedience and obstruction. Young men all over the country began to resist the draft, either by burning or by returning their draft cards. Others attempted to obstruct the war effort itself by shutting down military induction centers. By the end of 1967, a new type of hybrid demonstration had evolved. A classic peaceful political demonstration would be followed by a second demonstration that involved civil disobedience, some peaceful and some not. In October 1967, for instance, demonstrators occupied a University of Wisconsin building at Madison where Dow Chemical, the manufacturer of the napalm dropped in South Vietnam, was conducting employment interviews. In the same month, demonstrators tore down a fence at the Pentagon and some even entered the Pentagon building itself. While both the occupation of the building at Madison and the destruction of the fence at the Pentagon were in violation of law, they did not involve danger to human life. It was the police who inflicted wholesale beatings on protesters without distinguishing between peaceful protesters and those involved in illegal conduct. The press found the spectacle of hundreds of thousands of citizens taking to the streets to protest what they felt to be an unjust war to be a news story that was impossible to ignore. And when the demonstrations remained peaceful, the press coverage was respectful.

The press also played a large role in fomenting opposition to the war by its reporting on the fighting in Vietnam. While firmly in support of the war at its outset, the mainstream press slowly became more suspicious when administration claims of success were contradicted by the stories filed by reporters on the ground in Vietnam. The administration's formidable public relations resources attempted to portray a picture of military success in prosecuting the war, but often reporters in Vietnam found these reports overstated. In November of 1965, the American military publicized a "search and destroy" victory in the Central Highlands of Vietnam. But the press soon reported that, while at first the American assault had gone well, later the American troops had fallen into an ambush in which a total of 151 American soldiers were killed and another 121 wounded. When the military then reported these as only "moderate" casualties, the press cried foul. The media also reported that American "body counts" of enemy soldiers were sometimes inflated. One reporter claimed that an American battalion commander saw his original estimate of 160 enemy dead in a two-day operation near Pleiku climb to 869 before it was released to the press. And there were also news reports about the use of controversial weapons like cluster bombs and napalm that accentuated a darker side of combat that the military did not wish to emphasize.

Independent press reports also undermined the administration's story about the South Vietnamese army's role in the conflict. The Johnson administration projected an image of America helping a plucky emerging democracy bravely repel a foreign invasion. But press reports accurately pictured the South Vietnamese government as a corrupt regime engaged in a civil war with a foe that had impressive internal support. And press accounts often suggested that the South Vietnamese military was often more than willing to allow American troops to do the heavy fighting. Eventually the chasm between administration claims of success and press reports of setbacks created a "credibility gap" that also fueled opposition to the war at home.

The Supreme Court expanded the new approach to the First Amendment it had fashioned in the civil rights cases, applying it to new issues arising from protests against the war. The Court recognized the right of antiwar dissent in *Bond v. Floyd*,[43] invalidating an attempt by the Georgia House of Representatives to exclude civil rights leader Julian Bond from his seat in the House on the basis of his praise of the courage of protesters who burned their draft cards. And in *Ostereich v. Selective Service System*,[44] the Court invalidated a local draft board's practice of reclassifying the draft status of protesters to make them eligible for combat. *Watts v. U.S.*[45] reversed a conviction for making "a threat to take the life" of the president. Relying on the First Amendment's commitment to a wide-open debate, the Court ruled that the statute did not cover the defendant's statement at a protest that "[i]f they ever make me carry a rifle, the first man I want to get in my sights is LBJ."[46]

The Court also extended it decisions on peaceful protest to antiwar demonstrations. In *Bachellor v. Md.*,[47] convictions for "disorderly conduct" outside an army recruiting station were reversed. And the Court interpreted the First Amendment to protect expressive conduct as well as speech. In *Tinker v. Des Moines School District*,[48] the Court upheld the right of two high school students to wear black armbands to class to signify their opposition to the war. *Tinker* also represented an extension of free speech rights to students and endorsed the right of students to use school property for speech purposes. In *Spence v. Washington*,[49] the Court also reversed the conviction of a protester who had taped a peace symbol to an American flag he owned for violation of a statute criminalizing "improper use" of the American flag.

The Court also continued to use the doctrine of unconstitutional overbreadth to invalidate laws that chilled free expression. In *Gooding v. Wilson*,[50] Justice Brennan's majority opinion avoided the difficult free speech question of whether or not a protester had a First Amendment right to use profanity in addressing a police officer by ruling that regardless of the First Amendment status of the protester's statement, the conviction must fail because the statute invoked was so broad in its coverage as to deter other clearly protected protest.[51]

In the afterglow of the Warren Court, the Supreme Court, composed mostly of Warren-era appointees, continued to issue landmark free speech rulings. In 1971, the Court ruled in *Cohen v. California* that the state could not convict an antiwar protester of "disturbing the peace" for wearing a jacket displaying the message "Fuck the Draft" in the halls of a municipal courthouse.[52] And also in 1971, the Court issued a landmark free press decision when it invalidated the Nixon administration's attempt to prohibit the publication of the Pentagon Papers, a study of American involvement in Vietnam that reflected poorly on earlier administrations.[53]

These First Amendment–protected antiwar protest activities, together with independent press reports critical of the war effort, started to have an important political effect. The political change was incremental at first, but quickened after the Tet Offensive in January of 1968. The Viet Cong mounted attacks of surprising scope and intensity all over South Vietnam. Seventy thousand Communist troops poured into over one hundred cities, including Saigon and thirteen of the sixteen provincial capitols of the Mekong region. Four thousand Viet Cong attacked positions in Saigon, including the presumably impenetrable American embassy. And images of these attacks were piped directly into American living rooms on the evening news.

The American military was startled by this display of offensive strength by the enemy but was able to eventually frustrate the attacks. The American commander General William Westmoreland later argued that the enemy had taken a reckless gamble and lost, leaving itself vulnerable to American counterattack. He may have been correct in a military sense; the Viet Cong did absorb enormous losses of troops and were unsuccessful in fomenting insurrections by civilians in the South. But played against the background of three years of American claims that they had the Communists on the ropes, the Viet Cong's display during Tet of both offensive capacity and an undeterred determination to win persuaded most Americans that President Johnson's strategy had failed. Americans found it hard to reconcile images of an ongoing battle for the control of the American Embassy with administration predictions of an early victory in the near future. So, too, press photos of a South Vietnamese officer calmly blowing a suspected Viet Cong's brains out were difficult to reconcile with American ideals.

After Tet, the establishment press, which had for the most part followed the administration's lead in covering the war, subtly changed directions. Researchers later documented that before Tet network news programs featured government spokesmen five times more than opponents of the war; after Tet the split was about fifty-fifty.[54] That astute observer of public opinion Lyndon Johnson knew that an entirely new political context had formed when the highly respected CBS news anchor Walter Cronkite opined in February of 1968 that the war was fated to end in a "stalemate."[55] By March, support of the president's conduct of the war had dropped to 26 percent;[56] in that same month he narrowly escaped defeat in the New Hampshire Democratic primary by heretofore little-known "peace" candidate Senator Eugene McCarthy.

On March 31, 1968, President Johnson addressed the nation in a televised speech. He announced a cessation of the bombing of North Vietnam north of the twentieth parallel; he offered, without preconditions, to meet the North Vietnamese for negotiations whenever they were ready; and, finally, he announced that he would not be a candidate for the presidency in the 1968 election. Congress, the press, and the American people interpreted his speech as a dramatic turn in American policy, a prelude to the end of the war. It appeared that once again protest activities, combined with an independent press, had effected change on an important issue. But this prediction proved wrong. The Vietnam War continued for another seven years, during which more American soldiers died than in the years up to 1968. This prolongation of the war also had a speech dimension; it was, as we saw in chapter 2, in large part a product of President Nixon's effective use of the power of presidential speech.

A New Official First Amendment

The Warren Court's democratic self-government vision constituted the official interpretation of the First Amendment from roughly 1963 through 1971. But between 1968 and 1992, Republican presidents occupied the White House for all but four years. And the one Democratic president elected, Jimmy Carter, never had an opportunity to appoint a Supreme Court justice. Slowly the makeup of the Supreme Court changed, and in the process the tenor of the majority opinions became more conservative across a wide swathe of issues. Although the Supreme Court's rulings on the First Amendment attracted less attention than its rulings on issues like abortion and the rights of criminal suspects, the Burger and the Rehnquist Courts also quietly made important changes in First Amendment doctrine.

A new constitutional First Amendment challenger emerged, one that eventually became the official First Amendment. It saw the First Amendment as providing a bulwark against government censorship. The Warren Court's vision shared this anticensorship goal, but in addition believed that it should affirmatively support citizen political participation. A major difference was that the new conservative challenger did not see all government regulations limiting speech as presumptively unconstitutional. Instead, it divided regulations of speech into two categories. Those that were aimed at punishing the message of speech ("content-discriminatory," in the new jargon) were presumptively invalid. But regulations geared to advancing permissible government goals that accidentally limited speech were of less concern. The new approach believed that these "content-neutral" laws were permissible if they were reasonable in their limits on expression. A decision to limit the size of demonstrations protesting the invasion of Iraq would be unconstitutional if the government's goal was to silence dissent, but a "reasonable" regulation that limited the demonstration because it interfered with the "content-neutral" goal of efficient traffic circulation would be permitted.

We should keep in mind two facts in evaluating this new approach. First, the vast majority of regulations limiting speech rights are "content-neutral" in nature. Therefore, the new approach immunizes most regulation of speech from full First Amendment scrutiny. Secondly, a law regulating speech for a "content-neutral" reason curtails free speech rights just as much as a content-discriminatory statute does. The fact that a demonstration is curtailed because it interferes with traffic rather than because of its controversial message results in the same loss of free speech rights. And, as we will see in chapter 5, municipal officials often succumb to the temptation to articulate a content-neutral reason for concealing a content-discriminatory motive.

Slowly the new approach became the official Constitution on most First Amendment issues. In chapter 5 we will study in detail how the new approach eroded the right of groups to protest the war in Iraq. It also affected the right of political association. Here the greatest harm was done by the new conservative majority's refusal to hear cases challenging government investigations of free speech activist groups. The Court's refusal technically rested on a lack of standing under Article III, but its practical effect was to leave citizens' groups vulnerable to government spying and harassment.

The new majority also slowly eroded the central principle of the *New York Times v. Sullivan* decision. The case was not overruled, but the new majority created a large exception to its rule in cases involving "private figures," a term that it defined broadly.[57] But the greatest setback for the right of an independent press to inform the public came from the new majority's refusal to grant the press a First Amendment right to access government documents to obtain newsworthy information. We will also discuss this issue in chapter 4. And the new Supreme Court also dramatically cut back on the use of the doctrine of overbreadth.[58] Beyond the holdings of individual cases, there emerged a new attitude toward free speech disputes. The Warren Court had been suspicious of government claims that free speech had to be restricted in order for government to accomplish its objectives. It forced the government to justify its claims. The new conservative majority proved much more welcoming to such governmental claims.

But the Warren Court's self-government vision of the First Amendment did not disappear; it became the new challenger. While the Nixon and Reagan appointments led the Court away from the self-government principle, President Clinton's appointed justices Ruth Bader Ginsburg and Stephen Breyer were more receptive to it.[59] And some justices appointed by Republican presidents—like John Paul Stevens and David Souter—proved themselves more sympathetic to the arguments of free speech advocates than the presidents who appointed them had expected. Therefore, 5-4 decisions were common in First Amendment cases, as in other doctrinal areas.

There was another tilt to the Right during the second Bush administration. Chief Justice John Roberts's replacement of Chief Justice Rehnquist did not much change the ideological balance of the Court, but the appointment of extremely conservative Samuel Alito to replace the moderate conservative Sandra Day O'Connor certainly did. But change is a staple of constitutional practice, and President Obama's election in 2008 resulted in the appointment of Justice Sonia Sotomayor, who is expected to be sympathetic to the self-government model. Someday a new version of the self-government model may become the official First Amendment. That victory would constitute one more chapter in the history of intellectual and political struggle that characterizes our constitutional tradition.

4

Democracy in the Dark

The Press was protected so that it could bare the secrets of government and inform the people. Only a free and unrestrained press can effectively expose deception in government.
— Justice Hugo Black

We saw in chapter 2 how the power of presidential speech overwhelms the normal workings of our democratic decision-making process on national security issues. The smart response to this state of affairs is not to silence the president but to better support the opportunity for opposing voices to be heard. Unfortunately, as we saw in chapter 3, the current official First Amendment does not do that. In fact, First Amendment rights in the Burger, Rehnquist, and Roberts Court eras are significantly narrower than during the time of the Warren Court. On some issues, like the right of peaceful protest, which we will discuss in chapter 5, all we have to do is return to the Warren-era doctrine. But for other issues, we will have to expand the Warren Court's democratic self-government vision of the First Amendment to craft new doctrine for issues the Warren Court did not touch.

One such issue is government secrecy. Citizens can only perform their governing function if they are permitted access to the relevant facts. On some issues, like racial discrimination, the facts are readily available, but national security is a different case altogether. Here, most of the relevant information is controlled by the government, and the crucial First Amendment issue becomes whether the government has a right to withhold such information if it so chooses or whether the press has a right to access to it in order to inform the people. The current official First Amendment favors the government. We need a new interpretation. Otherwise, we are operating a democracy in the dark.

We need a First Amendment that makes sure the public is informed about how its government operates. The press plays a crucial role in this informing function by rooting out information that government officials would prefer to conceal from the public. Seymour Hersh's articles on the My Lai massacre in Vietnam drew public attention to a grisly aspect of the war in Vietnam that had not been featured in government press releases. So, too, the *New York Times'* publication of the Pentagon Papers alerted American voters to the fact that four different presidents had misled them about our involvement in Vietnam. And, of course, the Woodward/ Bernstein articles in the *Washington Post* played a major role in foiling President Nixon's attempt to cover up the Watergate scandal. More recently, in the Iraq War, we saw the same free speech phenomenon at work. Not only did the press bring the abuses of Abu Ghraib to public attention, but it was a *New York Times* story that alerted us to the fact that President Bush had authorized spying on American citizens in violation of congressional law.

Still, no one doubts that there is some information the government must keep secret. The Supreme Court long ago pointed out that democratic principles do not require disclosure of military secrets like "the sailing dates of transport ships or the number or location of troops."[1] This chapter, therefore, outlines the parameters of a national security information system that will provide citizens with the information they need to perform their duties as governors in a democracy without disclosing information that true national security concerns demand stay secret.

The Secrecy State

In the last half of the twentieth century, the amount of information declared off-limits to public scrutiny on national security grounds grew exponentially. Since 9/11 the pace of the movement towards secrecy has only quickened. Not only is more and more information "classified" as secret on national security grounds, but even nonclassified information is withheld because it relates to "critical infrastructure" or is considered "sensitive." In fact, the Bush administration claimed the right to withhold any information it chose on the ground that information that appears innocent to a layperson might have national security relevance as part of a larger "mosaic" of information. The logical consequence of this argument is that the government can withhold any information it wishes on the ground that it is impossible in advance to know what information might fit into such a mosaic.

Even "classified" information includes much information that there is no good reason to withhold from the public. There are a plethora of institutional pressures that favor unnecessary classification. The embarrassment to an agency from a failure to classify information that should have been classified is great; the fall-out from a decision to classify information that should be accessible to the public is nil. Also, secrecy gives the classifying agency an edge in its bureaucratic competition with other government agencies. And within the agency itself, the act of classifying supports the status system that separates the "in" group with access to secrets from the "out" group without such access.[2] Institutional inertia also works towards greater secrecy; once an original decision to classify documents has been made, related documents are routinely classified without a fresh evaluation of the need. And once information is classified, it continues to be kept secret long after the true need for secrecy disappears.

One reason presidents want control over access to national security information is that such contraol makes it easier to achieve their short-term policy goals. Presidential speech is more effective when the president can use classified information to bolster his position safe in the knowledge that his critics have no access to other information that might undercut his proposals. But the First Amendment is not intended to make the president's job of persuasion easier; its goal is to enable citizens to make up their own minds on the decisions that affect their lives.

Many readers may initially accept reports of excessive governmental secrecy as an example of the prudent maxim "better safe than sorry" in action. Maybe we have to accept an excess of secrecy to make sure that the true secrets are kept safe. But this instinctive reaction ignores important facts. First, history does not reveal any examples of vital secrets being disclosed because not enough information was classified. We have suffered injury to national security from espionage, but that's a completely different issue. Secondly, there is a palpable free speech cost to democratic decision making when information is unnecessarily kept secret. Not only does a lack of relevant information prevent voters from playing their constitutional role, but unnecessary secrecy often harms rather than protects national security. Experts tell us that high-level governmental decision making in the national security field often suffers from the institutional vice of "groupthink," the tendency of decision makers to undervalue dissenting views.[3] Public disclosure of as many of the relevant facts as possible enables more experts in and out government to analyze proposed policies and point out flaws they may contain. The run-up to the invasion of Iraq, discussed in chapter 3, is just one case in point. It is generally accepted now that we would have been better served if more information had been made available to the public about the doubts that experts had about whether Saddam Hussein posed an imminent threat to our national security.

There is a legitimate concern that disclosure of some national security information may alert enemies to facts they will use to harm us. It is here that the important task of determining what information must be kept secret and what information should be made public must take place. But, in the face of the many temptations that executive branch officials have to unnecessarily keep information secret, it makes no sense in policy terms to submit this important decision to their unmonitored discretion.

A First Amendment Right to Know

The American free speech tradition has primarily relied on the Free Speech Clause of the First Amendment text rather than the Press Clause or the Right of Political Association Clause, but there is no doubt that framers of the First Amendment saw an independent press as a bulwark of democratic government. In fact, at the time the Constitution was written, the freedom of the press was much better established in the American political tradition than freedom of speech. While only one postrevolutionary state constitution included a clause protecting freedom of speech, nine of the thirteen had provisions protecting freedom of the press. The framers of the First Amendment, as Justice Black reminds us in the quotation beginning this chapter, expected the press to play an important role in "informing" the people, including exposing government "deception."

The Supreme Court, in the afterglow of the Warren Court era, supported this informing function in the landmark case of *New York Times v. United States.*[4] The case involved the *New York Times'* decision to publish the Pentagon Papers. "The Pentagon Papers" was the popular name the press used to describe a multivolume secret study of American involvement in Vietnam from the end of World War II to 1968. It was compiled under the authority of President Johnson's secretary of defense, Robert McNamara, and documented the fact that four different presidents had misled the American public on our involvement in Vietnam. One of the study's authors, Daniel Ellsberg, leaked a copy to the *New York Times,* and the *Times* began publishing excerpts from the classified study in June of 1971. As we will see later in this chapter, this sort of "unauthorized leak" plays an important role in informing the public about information the government does not want them to know.

Even though the Pentagon Papers did not report on actions taken by his administration, President Nixon decided that unauthorized leaking could not be condoned and therefore ordered the Justice Department to obtain a court order banning further publication. The Department of Justice immediately asked the federal district court in Manhattan to enjoin further publication. The *Times* defended its right to publish and prevailed in the trial court but lost in the court of appeals, setting the stage for a ruling on the First Amendment by the Supreme Court. The government argued that the publication of the classified documents would seriously compromise national security, but was unable to specify serious concrete harms that publication would cause. The fact that the papers did not discuss actions after 1968 made it hard to prove such harm since the information did not pertain to present or future actions.

Seven individual justices filed opinions in the case, reaching their decisions by a variety of doctrinal routes. The bottom line was that six justices voted to dissolve the injunction, and the Court ordered that publication could continue. Three of the opinions are especially relevant to our discussion of the First Amendment and national security today because they constitute a dress rehearsal of today's debates about how judges should handle government claims for the need for secrecy on national security grounds.

Justice Harlan argued for a narrow scope of judicial review of the executive branch's claims:

[It] is plain to me that the scope of the judicial function in passing upon the activities of the Executive Branch . . . in the field of foreign affairs is very narrowly restricted. . . . The very nature of executive decisions as to foreign policy is political, not judicial. Such decisions are wholly confided by our constitution to the political departments. They are delicate, complex and involve large elements of prophecy. They are and should be undertaken only by those directly responsible to the people whose welfare they advance or imperil. They are decisions of a kind for which the Judiciary has neither aptitude, facilities, or responsibility. . . .[5]

Justice Harlan would limit judicial scrutiny to whether or not the papers dealt with matters within the president's power over foreign affairs. Since they clearly did, he felt that the claim of the need for secrecy should be upheld.

Justice Black's opinion argued that Harlan's approach ignored the fact that a central goal of the First Amendment is to expose government decisions to public scrutiny: "[The] Press was protected so that it could bare the secrets of government and inform the people. Only a free and unrestrained press can effectively expose deception in government."[6] Black understood that it is inevitable that governments will attempt to hide not only necessary secrets but also other information that only reflects poorly on the government politically. It is the press's job to expose this second type of government secret. Justice Brennan's opinion attached a method to Black's theory. He argued that prior restraints of the press should only be allowed upon "government allegation and proof that publication must inevitably, directly and immediately cause the occurrence of an event" seriously harming national security.[7] Since the government was unable to point to specific harms publication would bring about, Black and Brennan voted to dissolve the injunction.

The verdict of history is clear that the publication of the Pentagon Papers did not cause any concrete harm to national security. Almost twenty years after the decision, Erwin Griswold, the former Harvard Law School dean who had represented the government in the Supreme Court, admitted that he had "never seen any trace of a threat to the national security from their publication" or "even seen it suggested that there was such an actual threat."[8] On the other hand, there is no doubt that the publication of the Pentagon Papers did alert the American people to the well-established executive practice of deceiving the public when officials believe it serves their political interests to do so.

While the Pentagon Papers case was a rousing endorsement by the Supreme Court of the press's right to inform the people, I do not mean to claim that it has great precedential value in resolving the secrecy issues of today. The facts of the case involved an attempted government ban on the press's right to publish information already in its possession, an area where the First Amendment provides especially strong protection for the press. The most crucial free speech problems the press faces today do not involve such bans but rather involve the need to protect other press activities before and after publication, such as access to information in the government's possession and protection of the identity of sources of information.

But the decision is consistent with a larger view of the First Amendment that does resolve those issues. Justice Brennan put it well:

[T]he First Amendment embodies more than a commitment to free expression and communicative interchange for their own sakes; it has a structural role to play in securing and fostering our republican system of self-government. Implicit in this structural role is not only "the principle that debate on public issues should be uninhibited, robust, and wide-open," but the antecedent assumption that valuable public debate . . . must be informed. The structural model links the First Amendment to that process of communication necessary for a democracy to survive, not only for the communication itself, but also for the indispensable conditions of meaningful communication. [9]

This goal of the First Amendment is to ensure that public debates are not only free but also "informed." The First Amendment implies not only a right to speak but also a right to know.

This right to know arises in a variety of factual contexts. One extremely important one is the government's First Amendment duty to provide access to information in its possession relevant to issues of public interest. Such information is not the private property of the officials who control it; they possess it in the public trust. But the Burger Court ruled otherwise on that issue in the 1978 case of *Houchins v. KQED*.[10] *Houchins* involved a reporter's right to access to a county jail for the purpose of reporting on living conditions there. Although the case involved the narrow issue of access to a prison for prisoner interviews, it provided an opportunity for a face-off between a purely negative view of the First Amendment and one that saw the need for affirmative rights if it was to allow the press to perform its informing function. In *Houchins*, Chief Justice Burger argued that government officials had no affirmative constitutional duty to provide information to the press or public. Justice Stevens in dissent argued that news gathering was entitled to some constitutional protection:

Our system of self-government assumes the existence of an informed citizenry. . . . It is not sufficient, therefore, that the channels of information be free of governmental restraints. Without some protection for the acquisition of information about the operation of public institutions such as prisons by the public at large, the process of self-governance would be stripped of its substance. For that reason information gathering is entitled to some measure of constitutional protection.[11]

Justice Stevens believed that there was a need for First Amendment access to information controlled by the government in order "to ensure that the citizens are fully informed regarding matters of public interest and importance."[12] The Burger view won a narrow 4-3 victory, a result that needs to be changed.

Houchins involved access to prisoners held on governmental property. The issue of First Amendment access to documents in the government's possession has not come before the Court because Congress has made such access a statutory right. In 1966 Congress passed the Freedom of Information Act (FOIA) and then in 1974, in response to President Nixon's abuse of governmental secrecy, amended the act to dramatically expand citizen and press access to government records. FOIA is a good example of First Amendment structural legislation. It incorporates a First Amendment principle—here the right to access to governmental information—into a detailed legislative scheme. The legislature has institutional advantages over the judiciary in crafting comprehensive structural reforms. While the Supreme Court can better articulate constitutional principle, it is limited in its ability to create system-wide solutions by its focus on the individual case before it. Systemic legislative solutions informed by court-articulated constitutional principles are usually the best way to go. But it is important that the Court make clear that the statute is required by constitutional principle and is not merely a question of legislative discretion. The current Supreme Court has never given FOIA this necessary constitutional imprimatur.

The basic structure of FOIA is simple.[13] Any citizen has a right to a copy of any record in the possession of an agency of the United States government, unless the government can show that the record fits within one of nine exemptions. A citizen files a request with the agency and the agency then must expeditiously supply the information or deny the request citing statutory authority. If the requestor is dissatisfied, he or she can sue in federal district court to overturn the denial. The contested issue is usually whether or not one of the statutory exemptions applies. For instance, the agency might argue that the requested information is properly classified national security information (exemption 1), that it is protected by executive privilege (exemption 5), or that supplying the information would interfere with ongoing law enforcement procedures (exemption 7).

The agency has the burden of proof on qualifying for the exemption, and the judge, unlike in most reviews of administrative decisions, makes an independent decision about whether the government's claim is justified. To help the judge in this decision, the agency must provide a summary of the requested information and the specific exemption it feels justifies its refusal. Where sensitive information is involved, the judge can hold an *in camera* hearing (where the requestor's attorneys are not present) to make his or her decision. And while the judge is required to give substantial weight to the agency's views on matters of national security, the final decision is his or hers to make.

FOIA requests are the source of much of the information about public issues published in the press today. For instance, in chapter 5 we will discuss government surveillance of groups opposing the war in Iraq. What little knowledge we have about the extent of FBI surveillance is the product of FOIA requests that resulted in judicial orders that some of the records be made public. But after 9/11, FOIA requests rrelating in any way to national security were more likely to be denied. Government agencies were less willing to comply with the law and federal judges were less willing to make the independent judgment FOIA requires of them. Following the approach set out by Justice Harlan in his opinion in the Pentagon Papers case, they have been willing to accept almost any justification for denial that the government offers.

A good example of this excessive judicial deference to government national security claims is the case of *Center for National Security Studies v. Department of Justice*.[14] The case involved a large-scale roundup by the Immigration and Naturalization Service (INS) of legally admitted aliens soon after 9/11. We still know little about what actually transpired because the government has shrouded its actions in secrecy, a secrecy later endorsed by the District of Columbia Court of Appeals. Soon after the 9/11 terrorist attacks, the government arrested and jailed over one thousand legally admitted aliens. None of them was found to be involved in 9/11, although some were later charged with immigration violations and violations of American law not connected to terrorism. Two were held as material witnesses in terrorism investigations.

The Center for National Security Studies is one of the free speech activist groups we will discuss in chapter 5 that make democratic self-governance more than just a theory. They seek out the information necessary for informed democratic decision making. After the raids took place, the center filed a FOIA request asking for various pieces of information about the detainees. The request was denied by the government on several grounds, primarily that the information was covered by exemption 7 of FOIA in that its disclosure "could reasonably be expected to interfere" with law enforcement proceedings. The district court judge ruled that the government had not adequately justified its refusal to disclose two types of requested information, the names of the detainees and the names of their attorneys.[15] On appeal the Justice Department's case relied on affidavits by midlevel government officials claiming that the names of the detainees and their attorneys should be kept secret because disclosure might lead to terrorists discovering which of their members were in custody, and also might alert terrorists to the scope and progress of ongoing terrorist investigations.

While a good argument can be made that refusal to disclose the names of those being held as material witnesses in terror-related cases might be justified, there is no good reason to believe that the disclosure of names of detainees not even alleged to be connected with terrorism would give terrorists any useful information. These were innocent people with no connection to terrorism. So too the disclosure of the names of innocent arrestees would not seem to alert terrorist groups to whether their members had been arrested or to the "scope and progress" of the terrorist investigation, except in the trivial sense that the government had arrested the wrong people. The government argument is even weaker when used to justify refusal to disclose the names of the detainees' attorneys.

The government attempted to fill the hole in their case by use of the "mosaic" theory discussed above. Government attorneys contended that information that might seem trivial in importance to a lay person (like a federal district judge) might be placed in a larger mosaic of facts by an expert (like a terrorist) and found to yield important information. In other words, since any fact might conceivably be part of a sort of mosaic, all information can be withheld from the public. And this result, so alien to the spirit of FOIA (and the First Amendment), can be triggered by no more than a vaguely worded affidavit from a midlevel executive official.

The D.C. Circuit Court of Appeals accepted this novel theory in upholding the government's right to withhold the names of all detainees and their attorneys. The majority reasoned that "the judiciary is in an extremely poor position to second-guess the executive judgment in this key area of national security."[16] As the dissent succinctly put it, "This Court has converted deference into acquiescence."[17] In passing FOIA, Congress thought it important that the press and public be able to call attention to government abuses of authority in order that they might be remedied. With the benefit of hindsight, one suspects that the INS really had no good national security reason for withholding the information; rather, it had made a bureaucratic blunder in arresting so many innocent people and wanted to limit negative publicity and discourage lawsuits challenging the legality of the raids. The *Center for National Security Studies* decision is not only a defeat for FOIA and the First Amendment; it also is a defeat for a proper theory of separation of powers. Courts have a constitutional role to play in seeing that government obeys the law and the Constitution, a role that the D.C. Circuit Court of Appeals majority abdicated. We will return to this issue in chapter 6.

Necessary Secrets

Of course, there is a need for some government secrecy. Everyone agrees that certain information must be kept confidential. Accordingly, FOIA includes an exemption for properly classified documents. At a constitutional level, necessary secrecy is protected by the "state secrets" privilege and the broader doctrine of executive privilege. The "state secrets" privilege protects military and diplomatic secrets from public disclosure. The goal is to protect necessary secrets without providing the government an excuse to withhold information that can and should be part of public discourse. This has proved more easily said than done. Unfortunately, courts have been lax in protecting against such government chicanery.

The Supreme Court did not enforce the state-secrets privilege until 1953 in the case of *U.S. v. Reynolds*.[18] *Reynolds* involved a tort suit by the widows of three civilians who died in the crash of an air force B-29 that had been carrying secret electronic equipment. The plaintiffs alleged negligence and sought access to a government accident report on the crash to bolster their claim. Chief Justice Vinson's opinion upheld the government's refusal to disclose the report on the grounds that it contained "state secrets." The Court did make clear that the claim of privilege should not be made or accepted lightly. The Court said that the privilege must be formally claimed by a head of a department after "actual personal consideration."[19] But on the crucial issue of what role the

Court should play in determining the legitimacy of the claim, the *Reynolds* Court gave ambiguous advice: "The Court must itself determine whether the circumstances are appropriate for the claim of privilege, and yet do so without forcing a disclosure of the very thing the privilege is designed to protect."[20] The inference was that this could be done without the Court looking at the document in question. The Court thought that accepting the government's representations on the issue was the proper method in most cases.

This uncritical acceptance of government representations instead of judicial inspection of the document is misplaced in two ways. First, it assumes that disclosure to a federal district court judge who has taken an oath to support the Constitution represents a serious risk to national security. The federal courts are a coequal branch, and there is no reason to believe judges cannot devise procedures to keep a secret as well as bureaucrats. Secondly, it underestimates the temptation for government officials to manufacture national security justifications to withhold information that should be made public. As Sissela Bok points out in her book *Lying*, government officials sometimes feel entitled to dissemble. Officials often see "nothing wrong with telling untruths for what they regard as a much higher truth."[21] And of course, there is no higher truth in the minds of some officials in power than the righteousness of their national security goals.

Unfortunately, most courts since *Reynolds* have followed Chief Justice Vinson's example, accepting vaguely worded affidavits signed by agency officials as a substitute for looking at the document itself. The representations in *Reynolds* that disclosure of the documents would "seriously injure national security" came not from the secretary of the air force but from the judge advocate general of the air force, the official assigned to defend the litigation. After 9/11, the Bush administration invoked the state-secrets doctrine in a variety of lawsuits, arguing not just that they should not be required to produce the requested information but that the lawsuits should themselves be dismissed. For instance, when public interest groups sued telecommunication carriers for illegally aiding the National Security Agency's (NSA) program to spy on American citizens, the government successfully asked that the lawsuit be dismissed on the grounds that it would require disclosure of state secrets.[22] We will return to that case in chapter 6.

Courts should not force the executive branch to divulge military and diplomatic secrets, but neither should they accept all statements by government officials as gospel truth. To ensure that no more information is withheld than is necessary to avoid concrete injury to national security, judges should insist on reviewing the documents themselves to see if they endanger national security. Often this will require an *in camera* inspection.[23]

The subsequent history of the *Reynolds* litigation supports the wisdom of this more active judicial role. In the year 2000, thanks to the magic of the internet, a copy of the secret report in *Reynolds* became public. It contained no state secrets, but much evidence of negligence that would have embarrassed the agency and aided the plaintiffs in their suit.[24] Of course judges should listen to agency views; the fact that government officials sometimes claim privileges when they are not appropriate does not mean that there are not state secrets that judges should protect. But the final decision belongs to the judge. To leave that decision in the hands of interested government officials is to allow the executive branch to be the judge of its own case.

The related doctrine of executive privilege protects the confidentiality of a president's discussions with his advisors. Here the justification does not come from the subject matter of the conversations but rather from the need for the president to receive candid advice. The state-secrets privilege is limited in scope (only military and diplomatic secrets) but absolute in nature. Once the government shows that the information is within the privilege, the protection is absolute. Executive privilege, on the other hand, is broader in scope but only presumptive in nature. It extends beyond national security to cover the president's conversations with high-level aides on a variety of issues, but can be overcome by a showing that there is a substantial need to pierce the veil of secrecy.

Like the state-secret privilege, executive privilege was recognized by the Supreme Court rather late in our constitutional history. The issue arose in one of the most famous cases of the Vietnam era—*United States v. Nixon*.[25] Prosecutors demanded that President Nixon produce tapes that allegedly recorded conversations between Nixon and his aides in the Oval Office discussing how to cover up the Watergate burglary. Nixon refused on grounds of executive privilege. In an argument that anticipated the National Security Presidency model of separation of powers we discussed in chapter 1, Nixon's lawyers argued that the president, not the Court, should determine the scope of the privilege. The Supreme Court rejected this argument, but did recognize the narrow state-secret privilege for diplomatic and military secrets discussed

above and also an executive privilege not to disclose presidential conversations about other topics. But the Court also made it clear that the
executive privilege was not absolute in nature. "[W]hen the privilege
depends solely on the broad, undifferentiated claim of public interest in
the confidentiality of [presidential] conversations, a confrontation with
other values arises."[26] And it was for the courts, not the president, to
determine the qualified privilege's scope and weight. The Court then
ruled that on the facts of the case before it, Nixon's claim of privilege
succumbed before the prosecutor's need for the tapes in the trial of
Nixon's Watergate coconspirators. This ruling forced Nixon to give up
the tapes and eventually led to his resignation. More importantly for
our purposes, the decision reaffirmed the fact that in our constitutional
system it is the judges, not the president, who have the final say on the
Constitution's meaning.

President George W. Bush attempted to dramatically expand the doctrine of executive privilege during his term. When a congressional committee subpoenaed Bush aides Harriet Miers and Karl Rove to testify
about their role in the allegedly partisan firing of several U.S. attorneys
in 2007, the White House claimed not only that conversations between
the president and Miers and Rove were privileged but also that all other
conversations by aides in their official capacities fell within the privilege
whether or not they involved advice to the president. In fact, the Bush
administration claimed that Rove and Miers need not even appear before
the committees that subpoenaed them. This argument introduced the
same claims of presidential supremacy that the Supreme Court rejected
in *United States v. Nixon*. Eventually lawyers for Rove and Miers gave up
these extreme claims and agreed to testify under oath before the congressional committees.

Technically, presidential privileges are discussed under the rubric of
separation of powers, but we must remember that they also have a First
Amendment dimension. I have already argued that it is essential that
opposing voices be allowed to make their case against the prodigious
power of presidential speech to dominate the national security debate.
But the press is only willing to report what it sees as legitimate news
events, and lawsuits and congressional hearings qualify as such events. To
allow the president to use state-secrets and executive-privilege claims to
dismiss lawsuits or frustrate congressional investigations not only harms
the plaintiffs and lawmakers but also obstructs the press's right to inform
and the public's right to know.

Unauthorized Leaks

We have discussed three channels through which information that is relevant to an informed national security debate and that government would prefer to keep secret can come to public view. One is a FOIA request; another is evidence in a court proceeding; a third is evidence in a congressional hearing. All are important contributions to informed debate, but probably not as important as a final informal channel—the unauthorized "leak." Within the strictures of the secrecy state, the press often only obtains relevant national security information when a disgruntled employee provides information to a reporter without his or her superiors' authorization. Without such unauthorized leaks, the public would know much less about its government than is necessary in a healthy democracy. Our knowledge of the Watergate cover-up, the abuses at Abu Ghraib, and the National Security Agency's (NSA) secret spying on American citizens constitutes only a small sample of the much larger universe of important news stories that were in large part fueled by leaks. The First Amendment needs to protect the viability of this source of information as much as the others.

In providing that protection, we must keep in mind an elementary psychological fact: most sources demand confidentiality in return for their cooperation with the press. Mark Felt, the high-level FBI official who as "Deep Throat" guided the Woodward and Bernstein stories on Watergate, is only one example. Sometimes an informant acts without regard to future personal repercussions, but usually informants want the press to keep their identity secret. When government prosecutors then attempt to discover from the reporter the identity of the individual who leaked the confidential information, the stage is set for a constitutional face-off: Does the First Amendment protect reporters from government demands to reveal their sources?

This issue came before the Supreme Court in 1974 in the case of *Branzburg v. Hayes.*[27] The press argued that the First Amendment should be interpreted to provide reporters a shield—a "reporter's privilege"—because if reporters were forced under the threat of imprisonment to name their sources, much information necessary to public debate would be lost. In a 5-4 decision, the Court rejected that claim. At first glance it might appear appropriate that reporters should be required (like other citizens) to cooperate in the investigation and prosecution of violations of the law. But the issue becomes more complex when we consider the press's informing function. We also must take into account the problem of "authorized" leaking—the disclosure of secret information authorized by high-level executive branch officials. For instance, the same President Nixon who was so angry at Daniel Ellsberg's unauthorized leak of the Pentagon Papers felt no compunction about attempting to destroy Ellsberg's reputation by means of authorizing "leaks" of confidential information in the government's possession. With regard to unflattering information the government had gathered on Ellsberg, Nixon directed aides to "get it out. Leak it out. We want to destroy him in the press."[28]

The truth is that all government agencies use authorized leaks to disclose information to the press that they believe will help their policy goals. Unauthorized leaks by underlings only level the informational playing field by disclosing other information. But it is only unauthorized leaks that are prosecuted because the attorney general will not prosecute leaks authorized by his or her own administration.[29] Allowing prosecution of unauthorized leaks permits the government officials to punish the same acts that they themselves engage in.

The first step in resolving this conflict between the needs of an independent press and the need to enforce the criminal law is to only criminalize leaks in the most serious circumstances. The British have an "official secrets" law that makes it a crime to divulge almost any national security information. To its credit, our Congress has not followed the British precedent out of fear that it would deprive the public of too much important information that it needs to hear. Instead, Congress has only made it a crime to disclose information in a narrow category of situations like the intentional disclosure of the identity of a secret CIA agent.[30] In this situation not only the efficacy but also the life of the agent is at risk. Unfortunately, some courts have interpreted the vague language in a World War I espionage statute to dramatically expand criminal liability. The statute (18 U.S.C. 793(d)) makes it a crime for someone in possession of information "relating to the national defense" to transmit it to someone not authorized to receive it; one federal district court upheld under this statute the prosecution of the government official who transmitted classified information to a magazine.[31] After 9/11 Bush administration officials suggested that a companion statute, 18 U.S.C. 793(e), would even permit criminal punishment of the newspaper that published a leak. Under this theory, the *New York Times* decision to publish the Pentagon Papers would be transformed into a federal felony. Congress should repeal these antiquated statutes that would make the disclosure of almost any classified information a crime and should rely instead on a more focused approach that only authorizes prosecution in the most exigent circumstances.

But even where disclosure is a crime, the informing function requires that the First Amendment permit the press to protect the identity of its sources of information. Not only should the *Branzburg* decision be overruled, but Congress should also pass a federal "shield" law that will protect reporters against the threat of imprisonment for protecting the confidentiality of their sources. Critics argue that providing a reporter's privilege would constitute preferential treatment for reporters over other citizens, who must testify to information in their possession. This is true in a superficial sense since only reporters can claim the privilege, but this difference in treatment is not based on favoritism any more than the attorney-client privilege stems from a love of the legal profession. We grant a testimonial privilege to lawyers because we rightly believe that they need confidential information from their clients to do their job properly. The reporter's privilege is based on the same reasoning. We want the press to provide us with information relevant to public affairs; often they can only obtain this information by promising confidentiality. Therefore, it's in the public interest to protect that confidentiality.

But even advocates of the need for a federal reporter's privilege disagree on its content. The most popular position seems to be something akin to the "qualified" privilege that Justice Stewart called for in his *Branzburg* dissent.[32] This would allow a judge to decide which confidences to protect and which not to protect after considering all the relevant factors. The problem here is that such a judicial balancing long after the promise of confidentiality was given provides the confidential source no assurance that the privilege will be respected at a later date. It's exactly that assurance that produces the disclosures that the First Amendment favors. That's why most testimonial privileges like the attorney-client privilege are absolute rather than qualified in nature. A qualified reporter's privilege will give the wrong message not only to the source but also to the reporter and his or her employers. Asserting qualified privileges is both risky and expensive. Reporters and newspapers might well decide that the safer and less expensive course is to avoid investigative reporting altogether.

There is also the issue of who can claim the privilege. Here the question is how broad a definition to give the term "reporter." We limit the attorney-client privilege by confining it to individuals licensed by the state, but there is no such clear demarcation designating who qualifies as a reporter. This issue becomes even more important in the internet era when the informing function is increasingly performed by individuals not connected to the mainline press. There is always the danger that someone who wishes not to give information to the grand jury will attempt to qualify for the reporter's privilege. On the other hand, it would seem short-sighted to limit the privilege to reporters for the mainline press in an era when so much investigation is performed by academics, nonfiction writers, and bloggers on the internet. Artful drafting should be able to solve this problem. The key element should be whether the claimant of the privilege can show that he or she was investigating a newsworthy event for dissemination to the public.

Press Access to War Zones

Another area where there should be First Amendment–mandated press access to newsworthy information involves military operations. Not all information relevant to national security debates can be gleaned from government files or the testimony of government officials. Often it is necessary for the press to take a first-hand look at how military operations are progressing in the field. We saw in chapter 2 that it was the contrast between government reports on the progress of the Vietnam War and the reports filed by correspondents in Vietnam that alerted the American people to the failure of President Johnson's policies. Therefore, the First Amendment right of access to information must extend to independent press access to war zones. Unfortunately, to this point, Congress and the courts have allowed press access to be treated as a privilege that the military can grant or deny as it pleases. Not surprisingly, the military uses this discretion to influence the way the press tells the story.

Reporters now look back to the Vietnam era as a golden age in the history of the American press. Such nostalgia tends to ignore the fact that the press almost unanimously supported the war until it became obvious that it was not turning out as advertised. Yet there was a lot of good reporting of the Vietnam War, much of it comprised of factual reports that undercut optimistic government pronouncements of victory in the near future. And these reports played a large role in changing the American public's perception of the war in the later sixties and early seventies. Conservative critics later charged that the press was one large reason why we "lost" in

Vietnam, but such charges are only examples of the well-known human tendency to blame the messenger. The American military was stalemated by the North Vietnamese, not the press.

The press was able to perform its informing function in Vietnam because of the press policy that the Johnson administration adopted there. While press censorship was briefly considered as an option in Vietnam,[33] the administration finally decided that censorship of the press was politically and practically impossible in a place as open as Vietnam. Therefore, the military implemented a strategy that included full access for reporters, complemented by a well-functioning war propaganda operation. There were not only appeals to reporters' patriotism, as when Vice-President Hubert Humphrey urged reporters to "give our side the benefit of the doubt,"[34] but also free access to war zones, priority for military transportation, and provision of food and shelter. In return, reporters agreed to abide by military guidelines to prevent gaffes like premature notice to the enemy of the movement of troops.

In the aftermath of Vietnam, American military leaders regretted this policy of free access and took steps to ensure that the Vietnam press experience was never repeated in later military operations. First in Grenada and Panama in the eighties, and later in the first Gulf War after Iraq's invasion of Kuwait, the military slowly refined a media relations strategy that dramatically curtailed the role of an independent press. In the first Gulf War, this strategy was centered on the institution of a "pool" system for reporters. News organizations would submit names of reporters to be included in press pools that were allowed access to the war zone on the condition that they share the information they gained with other reporters left back in Saudi Arabia. The military kept two controls on the "pooled" media. First, they were always escorted by military "public affairs officers" who steered the reporters to stories the military wanted covered and monitored all interviews the reporters had with soldiers. Secondly, all stories, photos, and film coming from the pools were subject to "security review," a polite name for government censorship. While the military censors did not actually forbid the publication of much information under security review, long delays in processing the reviews resulted in much information becoming too stale for publication. Reporters who did not agree to become part of a pool were called "unilaterals." In Vietnam, independent reporters could count on military assistance as to travel, food, lodging, and interviews. Now unilaterals were viewed by the military as well as their pool colleagues as troublemakers who refused to play by the rules. They were given no assistance; instead, they had to worry about being arrested for being in areas closed off to unauthorized personnel.

The military press strategy in Gulf War I also included a sophisticated Pentagon media campaign featuring square-jawed young officers in uniform giving glowing reports of American success on the battlefield and government-produced media film clips celebrating "smart bombs" that always hit their military targets without "collateral damage" to civilians. This was the sanitized, but misleading, picture of the war Americans saw on their television screens. It was only after the war that we were told that the overwhelming majority of bombs dropped were conventional bombs that often caused indiscriminate damage.

For the invasion of Iraq in 2003, the military further refined its media relations policies by introducing the concept of "embedded" reporters. Now reporters would not be outsiders reporting on the war but integral parts of the combat units fighting the war. Many reporters thought it was an offer too good to refuse: "We were offered an irresistible opportunity: free transportation to the front line of the war, dramatic pictures, dramatic sounds. Great quotes. Who can pass that up?"[35] The military wagered that reporters living day to day with soldiers would eventually adopt the soldiers' positive view of the war. This proved usually to be the case; most embedded reporters were eager to support their soldier comrades' dangerous mission by filing flattering stories, and those few who filed stories that were viewed as negative were quickly reprimanded by members of their units for their disloyalty to the group. In sum, while some stories embarrassing to the military were published by embedded reporters, the coverage on the whole was usually extremely sympathetic to the military view. Television coverage was also biased toward the military's view. Not only did the networks feature stories by embedded reporters and use film clips supplied by the Pentagon, but in 2008 the *New York Times* published a report that showed that even the supposedly "objective" military experts employed by the networks to comment on the war's progress had been vetted and briefed by the military. These retired military officers, almost all of whom had connections with military contractors, used their neutral status to sell the Pentagon's view of the invasion and the insurgency to unsuspecting viewers. When the news product is a combination of visuals created by government-sponsored reporters commented upon by government-briefed experts, the result is that the public knows little about the war other than what the government wants it to know.

There is nothing the First Amendment can do to prevent the press from adopting a progovernment bias. An independent press must even be free to accept the government's offer to function as a public relations unit for the military. Otherwise it is not independent. But the First Amendment should have some impact on the military's treatment of reporters who choose to remain free of governmental control. The treatment of independent reporters in Iraq is a good example of a situation the First Amendment should not tolerate. In Iraq, the military attempted to shut down independent coverage of the war. A 75-mile "military exclusion zone" was established around the war zone. Unembedded reporters who entered this zone were harassed and expelled. The military took the position that the "embedded" program fulfilled its duties to the press and that independent reporters were at best unnecessary distractions and at worst a threat to the safety of the troops. The combination of government control of officially sanctioned reporters and exclusion of independent reporters resulted in a highly slanted view of the way the war was actually conducted.

The press and the military both have a job to do in times of war, but often their missions conflict. It makes no more sense to allow the military to mandate the rules of press access than it does to allow the press to direct the positioning of troops. Here we need to adopt Justice Stevens's position in his *Houchins v. KQED* dissent that the First Amendment grants the press protection in its news-gathering activities. This constitutional principle should then be implemented by congressional legislation modeled on the Freedom of Information Act (FOIA) that would set out the parameters of press access to military operations. There should be a transparent process for certifying correspondents. Transportation and logistical support should be provided at a fair price so as to maintain press independence. As in Vietnam, there should be guidelines that protect against the disclosure of certain confidential information and sanctions for reporters who violate the guidelines. But the military should not have authority to review and edit reports of certified reporters prior to publication. So, too, the legislation should set out situations in which press access can be limited. For instance, press activities should not be allowed to endanger the lives of troops, but that rationale should not be allowed to unreasonably block access. Most importantly, there must be some officer independent of the military designated to quickly resolve disagreements that arise. The military should not be allowed to treat press access as a privilege it can grant or deny as it deems fit. We should not expect the military to like the idea that an independent press can publish stories critical of its performance, but, as the old saying goes, "War is too important to leave to the generals."

The Internet Era

The fact that the press has historically played an important role in our democratic process does not mean that it has always played it well. The sad truth is that the mainline press has usually been an uncritical supporter of any use of military force a president proposes. We saw this phenomenon both in the first years of the Vietnam War and again when President Bush decided to invade Iraq. In both cases, it was only when the prospect of a quick victory disappeared that the press began to scrutinize government policy. This should not be surprising; the mainline press has a built-in bias in favor of the government's views on foreign affairs. This bias comes not from any necessary ideological stance but from the fact that the mainline press has traditionally embraced a self-image of "objectivity" that determines its methods of operation. It believes that an objective press must print what government officials say. Since the president and his surrogates speak often and in concert on national security issues, press coverage tends to favor government's chosen narrative. Of the 414 network news stories on the run-up to the Iraqi invasion aired between September 2002 and February 2003, only thirty-four originated from outside the government.[36] Of course, the press also publishes opposing opinions from what it deems to be responsible critics, but it defines this group narrowly to include only those who oppose the tactics employed by the administration rather than those who oppose its goals. Consider how many times an expert has been interviewed on network television arguing that Iran as a sovereign state has as much right as India, Pakistan, Israel, or the United States to determine its own nuclear policy. My educated guess is that no such interview has ever appeared. And if an opposition figure does speak out against administration policy, the political reality is that a single contrary opinion will never attain the traction necessary to support an alternative narrative for citizens to adopt against the waves of proadministration speech. Domestic commentators outside the mainstream are mostly ignored as eccentrics, and the press policy of neutrality is not extended to foreign opponents of administration policy; the press is happy to side with American officials in factual disputes with foreign leaders. And there are also financial incentives that impact press coverage. Television news is a very profitable and competitive business, and war coverage draws large audiences at a low cost since almost all of the costs of production are borne by the government itself.

This is an unwelcome fact for those of us who want a more open and informed debate on issues as important as those affecting national security. The combination of a powerful presidency and a complaisant press is a toxic one for the hopes of democratic government. But it is not a problem that the First Amendment can rectify directly. If we want an independent press with the freedom to oppose the government, we have to allow the possibility of an independent press that supports the government. The First Amendment cannot tell the press what to say.

Fortunately, this is an area where technology and market forces may play a very positive First Amendment role. The growth of the internet is dramatically transforming the way Americans receive their news in a manner that might pay large dividends from a free speech perspective. Young people no longer read the print media or watch network news shows for political information; instead, they rely on the internet for political information. And political websites and blogs provide their readers with a cornucopia of political views unrestrained by the professional objectivity that constrains their mainline competitors. It is true that websites and blogs tend to be heavy on commentary rather than neutral analysis, but the internet's capacity to provide a large variety of views, amplified by links to other sites and the opportunity for instantaneous reader response, suggests that democratic debate will be not only changed but changed for the better.

There is a downside to this dramatic transformation of the American press. First, there is the draining away of financial resources from the mainstream press, revenues that support serious investigative reporting we need. While internet bloggers have uncovered important new facts, usually the internet discusses information already published by the same newspapers it is driving out of business. Also, Cass Sunstein has pointed out the temptation for internet users to choose to only visit internet sites that share their views. This could lead to a fragmentation and polarization of political views that is unhealthy for democratic government.[37]

But even Sunstein agrees that the new paradigm is likely to be better from a democratic perspective than the old regime. First, as we have pointed out, the "objective" press turns out not to have been so objective after all, especially on national security affairs. And while a more decentralized news industry may provide less broad debate between competing views than we see, for example, on the op-ed page of the *New York Times*, it does provide more venues for citizens to present their views and encourages debate within more particularized political perspectives. And Sunstein also admits that a significant percentage of internet readers appear to insist on getting their news from sites with differing political slants.

So too, it would be premature to count out the mainstream press; it may be revitalized by the new ideas that percolate up from internet sites. Even sober institutions like the *New York Times* are restructuring their operations to become more web-friendly publications. Newspapers may still develop a business model that will allow them to thrive in the internet era. This chapter has discussed the press, and the next chapter will discuss the role of free speech activists, but it is increasingly clear that the divide between the two is eroding as activist groups and nonprofits are able to communicate directly with the public via the internet. And these groups, perhaps aided by foundations, may well reduce the deficit in investigative reporting that the financial decline of newspapers has caused. It has been free speech activists like the Center for National Security Studies and the ACLU who have filed the FOIA lawsuits attempting to pierce government secrecy since 9/11.

We really do not know what the future holds for the traditional press and its internet competitors. Our public culture will almost certainly be more polycentric than before. We will be exposed to a greater variety of political views than in the era before the internet explosion. To the extent that this makes it more difficult for the government to manage public debate, it will be a healthy change. But the existence of views opposing government policy on national security is not enough to create a meaningful debate. We also need activist groups to nurture and publicize those ideas. The First Amendment's role in supporting these groups' efforts to perform that important function is the topic of the next chapter.

%% 5 %%

Free Speech Activists

*Almost always, the creative dedicated minority has made
the world better.*   —Martin Luther King Jr.

We saw in chapter 2 that the president's symbolic role in our political system, combined with his control over national security information and his unparalleled access to the media, permit him to dominate debate on national security issues. Chapter 4 then argued that one way to reestablish the proper balance would be to support the press's ability to maximize the flow of national security information to the public. But the press can never imagine, nurture, and publicize the alternative ideas on national security and other issues that democratic debate requires. Its primary role is reactive rather than creative; the press reports and comments on the actions and ideas of others. It is activist groups that nurture the new ideas that major political parties later adopt and instill as national policy.

The civil rights movement provides us with one clear example of the way free speech activists play this catalytic role. The facts of segregation were out in the open for everyone to see, but it was not until African-American citizen groups like the National Association for the Advancement of Colored People (NAACP) and the Southern Christian Leadership Council (SCLC) took the lead in the fight to end segregation that the tide of history turned. Eventually the northern press supported civil rights reform and the Democratic Party under John F. Kennedy adopted it as part of its legislative program in 1963. It was President Lyndon Johnson—partly by adroit use of presidential speech—who finished the cycle by bringing about the passage of the landmark Civil Rights Act of 1964 and the Voting Rights Act of 1965. But we should never forget that both Kennedy and Johnson were reacting to political pressures that activists like Martin Luther King Jr. had set off many years earlier with a boycott of segregated buses in Montgomery, Alabama.

We saw a similar phenomenon during the Vietnam War. The major political parties and the mainline press were strong backers of the war at the outset. It was activist groups like Students for a Democratic Society (SDS) and the Committee for a Sane Nuclear Policy (SANE) that pointed out the war's tension with American democratic ideals and created new forms of protest like "teach-ins" to mobilize opposition. It was only much later that a majority of the Democratic Party and the many members of the press joined them.

Throughout American history this catalytic function has been performed by activist groups—abolitionists, suffragettes, labor organizers, environmentalists, and human rights advocates. And it is also important to remember that free speech activism is not a monopoly of the Left; conservative activists have used similar tactics to successfully advocate their views on abortion issues and the punishment of drunk driving. Not all ideas proposed by free speech activists are (or should be) adopted by the larger political system. But even when their ideas are rejected, their participation enriches democratic debate by forcing defenders of the status quo to respond to their arguments.

But free speech activism, so essential to democracy, is a very fragile social organism; it seldom makes sense from a dollars and cents perspective. And it is especially vulnerable to government repression because government agencies can always harass activists under the cover of investigating possible illegal conduct. Therefore, if we agree with Justice Brandeis that "the greatest menace to freedom is an inert people,"[1] we need a First Amendment that offers activists a realistic opportunity to do their job.

The Right of Peaceful Protest

One important way to allow activists to be heard is to allow them access to the streets and parks where they can plead their case to the public and the press. We saw in chapter 3 how the Warren Court interpreted the First Amendment to include a right to such access. Peaceful public protest became the civil rights movement's single most potent weapon in its struggle for political change. The Montgomery bus boycott, the "sit-ins" at segregated department stores in Nashville and other southern cities, the "freedom rides" throughout the South, the Birmingham protests, and the march on Washington have all taken well-earned places of honor in American political history. So, too, the "teach-ins" and the mass marches against the war in Vietnam played an essential catalytic role in alerting the American public to the negative consequences of sending large numbers of troops to Vietnam. Both the civil rights movement and the antiwar protests are eloquent testimonials to the importance of peaceful protest in effecting political change by demonstrating that large numbers of citizens care enough about the issue to rise from their sofas to personally participate in a political event.

It is important to remember that a demonstration is more than its message; marches and rallies also nurture solidarity among participants who discover that the issue so personally important to the individual participant is equally important to tens (or hundreds) of thousands of others. A successful march or rally raises hopes, convincing both participants and spectators that there may well be enough political energy available not only to call for change but to make it happen. This sort of organizational hope is essential to successful efforts at political change.

As late as February 2003 it looked as though this long tradition of political protest would continue after 9/11. A large march was planned that month in New York to protest President Bush's decision to invade Iraq; it was planned to coincide with similar demonstrations all over the world in cities like London, Berlin, Amsterdam, Copenhagen, Madrid, Dublin, Sydney, Athens, and Tel Aviv. The demonstration in New York would be especially significant because New York had been the primary target of the 9/11 attacks. A mammoth New York protest against the Bush administration's decision to invade Iraq without United Nations authorization would be a strong rejoinder to the administration's argument that the Iraq invasion was necessary to prevent future terrorist attacks.

The organizing group, United for Peace and Justice, contacted the New York Police Department (NYPD) in January of 2003 to arrange for the permits necessary for a march and rally on February 15. The proposed march would begin at a plaza near the United Nations building and would proceed past the UN building and the United States Mission to the United Nations and terminate with a large rally on the Great Lawn in Central Park.

The organizers of the march pointed out to the NYPD that the symbolism of a march before the United Nations was especially important since it was to the UN that Secretary of State Colin Powell had addressed his claims that Iraq was hiding weapons of mass destruction. It was also the UN to whom arms inspector Hans Blix had reported that his team's inspection had not uncovered any such weapons. Now it was time for the UN to hear from ordinary New Yorkers.

The NYPD refused to grant permits for the proposed march or for any march in the city of New York that day. Instead, it offered to permit a rally on a side street within view of the United Nations building. The demonstration's organizers filed suit in federal district court alleging that the refusal to permit the march was a violation of their First Amendment rights to use the streets as a public forum for peaceful protest. After some discovery, briefing, and oral argument, federal judge Barbara Jones upheld the NYPD's refusal to allow a march that passed in front of the UN building or anywhere else in Manhattan.[2] In the body of her opinion, Judge Jones conceded that the proposed march was protected free speech activity, but then set out the new narrow formula for regulating demonstrations that the conservative Burger and Rehnquist Courts had made the new official First Amendment. It was a formula that gave municipal officials a good deal of discretion to allow no more dissent than they wished to allow:

> [T]he government may impose reasonable restrictions on the time, place, and manner of protected speech, provided the restrictions "are justified without reference to the content of the regulated speech, that they are narrowly tailored to serve a significant governmental interest, and that they leave open ample alternative channels for the communication of the information." *Ward v. Rock v. Racism*, 491 U.S. 781, 791 (quoting *Clark v. Community for Creative Non-Violence* (1984))[3]

The march's organizers immediately appealed Judge Jones's decision to the federal appellate court for the Second Circuit. They did not contest Judge Jones's statement of the applicable rule but argued that she made three errors in applying it. First, the refusal to grant the permits was not justified "without reference to the content of regulated speech" since the city regularly granted permits to large marches, like the St. Patrick's Day parade, that communicated less controversial messages. Even if there were legitimate safety concerns to be considered for a march passing the UN, the refusal was not "narrowly tailored" since there were several effective ways of protecting the UN that were less intrusive on the free speech rights of marchers. The NYPD could just station a line of officers to "buffer" any contact between the marchers and the UN building. And, the stationary rally proposed by the city as a substitute did not constitute an "ample alternative channel" for communication of the group's message. Many potential marchers would stay home rather than be forced to stand in freezing temperatures in a rally that would have much less symbolic power than a march past the United Nations building. A stationary rally also would provide fewer of the good "visuals" that attract the media coverage the organizers needed to garner to make the demonstration politically effective.

The Second Circuit upheld Judge Jones's decision, ruling that she had accurately stated the applicable constitutional principles and appropriately applied them to the factual context before her.[4] The court accepted the city's argument that the reason they allowed the St. Patrick's Day parade and not the antiwar march had nothing to do with the respective messages of the marches. The St. Patrick's Day parade, the court pointed out, was planned over a full year with many meetings with the parade organizers to make sure things went smoothly. In contrast, the organizers of the February 15 event had only given the police three weeks' notice and were not able to specify how many people might attend the march, their estimates ranging from 50,000 to 150, 000 people. Therefore, the difference in treatment was not due to the message but to the "manner" of the proposed marches. The St. Patrick's Day parade was a "regular, annual" event with which the police department felt comfortable, and the antiwar march was a single event with uncertain attendance. The court seemed to blame the organizers of the march for not notifying the police a year in advance, well before the president had announced his decision to invade Iraq.

The Second Circuit also agreed with Judge Jones's determination that the limitation on the marchers' free speech rights was "narrowly tailored." To the plaintiffs' suggestion that the police allow the march but provide a buffer between the parade and UN property, Judge Jones had relied heavily upon the testimony of Assistant Chief Michael Esposito, who testified that such a buffer would be insufficient for a march of one hundred thousand people: "That's just an awful lot—amount of people. If they at one time did something or if somebody in the group had a device, I don't know how we would be able to stop it with that amount of people or see anything."[5] Judge Jones and the Second Circuit both docilely accepted this claim that the police could not protect the United Nations building from a march that was organized to support United Nations authority. Of course, there is always the danger of random vandalism, but the proper First Amendment response to vandalism is to arrest the vandals, not penalize the peaceful protesters. Assistant Chief Esposito's argument that someone on the march would "have a device" to explode also seems off the mark. If someone wanted to bomb the United Nations, they had no need of a march; they could walk up to the building anytime they wanted. And if they wanted to explode a device in a large crowd, a stationary rally would make an even better target than a march in which people are moving. But instead of asking the hard questions the First Amendment should require, the court accepted all the NYPD's claims as true. It also pointed out that the Supreme Court in the *Ward* case relied upon by Judge Jones had made clear that the "narrowly tailored" restrictions required by the First Amendment need not be "the least restrictive or least intrusive means of regulating speech."[6]

The Second Circuit also saw the substitute stationary rally near the UN building as providing the organizers with "ample alternative channels" to communicate their message. It agreed with Judge Jones's view that the First Amendment does not entitle protesters to "access to every or even the best channels of communication for their expression,"[7] nor does it "guarantee news publicity for speakers. . . ."[8] Both Judge Jones and the Second Circuit demonstrated the same deference to government authority we saw in the District of Columbia Circuit Court's opinion in the *Center for National Security Studies* case discussed in chapter 4. Judge Jones commented, "The Court will not second-guess or substitute its judgment for that of the NYPD."[9] It is true that the First Amendment does not require courts to second-guess government policy judgments, but it does require the judge rather than the police to make the final balance of constitutional values.

Having been rebuffed by the Second Circuit's upholding of Judge Jones's decision, the march organizers had little choice but to proceed with the demonstration the police had designed for them. This consisted of a stationary demonstration on First Avenue near the UN building. The organizers probably thought that the worst was behind them, but they were mistaken. Over a hundred thousand people arrived in Manhattan to protest the war, but they found that the police blocked the routes that gave most direct access to the demonstration site, limiting access to a few entrances. The resulting back-up at the designated entrances created a situation where large groups of demonstrators were milling around inter-sections in midtown Manhattan, often spilling out into the streets. The police responded by insisting that all protesters stay on the sidewalks even where there was no room for them to stand. The police then enforced this command by pushing the crowd back with a phalanx of mounted police armed with batons. The police also used pepper spray and made numer-ous arrests of citizens who were guilty of no more than not being able to get out of the way. Here is a description of the chaos that ensued, related by a lawyer who attended the demonstration with his five-year-old son:

> 52nd street was blocked off. All of a sudden a troop of mounted offi-cers moved into the crowd, the horses' high-stepping and moving their flanks to the side, and went through the peaceful and standing crowd, who were not blocking anything. The result was that people were pushed out of the way and falling bodies came towards me. My son and I were knocked over, I onto my back and he, fortunately, on top of me, but a woman in front of him was about to fall and crush him when I used my arms to deflect her to the side so that she did not injure him.[10]

Those lucky enough to reach the demonstration site found that they were forced to stand in holding "pens" formed by metal tubing; demonstrators were not allowed to leave the pens without being escorted from the dem-onstration site. This not only prevented the informal interaction between demonstrators that has always been a feature of demonstrations but also required protesters to stand in the fifteen-degree cold for hours without access to toilets. Not only were later arrivals unable to hear the speeches; many found themselves trapped in the pens. Here is the description one protester gave to the New York Civil Liberties Union:

> We couldn't really hear the speakers, but we could finally see where the stage was, and that people were speaking. . . . When we were about to leave, probably about an hour later, we noticed that the block had completely filled in. The crowd was pressed up so tight against the metal barricades that a woman was getting hysterical. She shouted "you have to let me out! I want to go home! I want to go home!" "Stop pushing" said the officer. "I'm not pushing," she answered. "I'm get-ting pushed."[11]

The NYPD's handling of the February 2003 antiwar demonstration proved to be a bellwether for the way other municipalities dealt with protests in the post-9/11 era. New York City hosted the 2004 Republican Convention, an event that attracted a large number of demonstrators against government policy. The NYPD employed basically the same approach that had been approved by the Second Circuit for the February 2003 demonstrations. Boston hosted the 2004 Democratic Convention at the Fleet Center. Again municipal officials gave little attention to the First Amendment rights of protesters, and again the federal courts condoned their actions.[12] Boston instituted both a "hard" and a "soft" protected zone around the Fleet Center. The hard zone was open only to approved users like delegates, and since this was the only area close to the Fleet Center itself, protesters were never allowed to get close to the real action. In theory protesters were to be allowed in the soft zone, but in practice this proved illusory; the city refused to allow any march to pass by the entrance to the Fleet Center during the days when the convention was actually convened.

Protesters were not allowed free access to the streets near the center; instead, they were relegated to a government-created "Demonstration Zone" (DZ). The federal judge who heard the case alleging First Amendment violations visited this site and described the DZ as "a grim, mean, and oppressive space" that reminded him of a prison.[13] He was not even sure that the delegates would even be able to see demonstrators within the DZ; certainly there would be no chance to pass literature to delegates because they would be separated by an eight-foot-high chain link fence covered with an opaque wire mesh to prevent demonstrators from throwing liquids at delegates or police. "Let me be clear: the design of the DZ is an offense to the spirit of the First Amendment. It is a brutish and potentially unsafe place for those who wish to exercise their First Amendment rights."[14] Unfortunately, after voicing these lofty civil-libertarian sentiments, the judge upheld the DZ as a reasonable security precaution. Like the judges in New York, he felt that the new official First Amendment did not permit him to "second-guess" municipal authorities.[15] Similar strategies were again used by the host cities for the 2008 party conventions, Denver and St. Paul. Each city created a security zone around the convention site that was off-limits to protest as well as an authorized free speech demonstration area more removed from the main action. Some marches were allowed, but never at a time or a place where they would distract delegates or the television networks from the official convention proceedings. The police in St. Paul actually directed one group of demonstrators on a route that led away from the convention center.

Is Peaceful Protest an Endangered Species?

Even though peaceful political protests like mass marches and rallies have played an important role throughout American political history, they have become increasingly rare events. There may well be sociological reasons why Americans appear less likely to take to the streets to oppose government policies than in earlier times. It clearly does not reflect a national apathy towards politics; there is plenty of opposition to the policies of whatever government is in power. Perhaps Americans today are more private in their behavior than in the sixties and seventies and prefer to oppose government policy on the internet instead of engaging in mass marches. Most of the participants in the sixties marches were under thirty and enjoyed confronting authority; now it may be that members of that age group of Americans have adopted a more muted personal style. But, leaving aside these possible sociological explanations as beyond my expertise to judge,[16] I would like to propose two facts of a more legal nature that have contributed to the decrease in peaceful protest on national security issues in the post-9/11 era.

The first explanation involves a change in the way governments viewed public protest after 9/11. Municipal governments have never enthusiastically welcomed protest because marches inflict financial costs that officials would prefer to avoid, but once the Supreme Court in the 1960s endorsed the protesters' rights to use streets and parks for political expression, most municipalities worked with protest organizers to minimize inconvenience to other citizens. This attitude changed after the mass protests against the World Trade Organization (WTO) at its meeting in Seattle in 1999.[17] That year large numbers of protesters (conservatively estimated at forty thousand) of all ages went to Seattle to protest WTO trade policies that they saw as maximizing corporate profit at the expense of poor countries, workers, and the environment.[18]

The WTO protests involved three types of protesters. By far the largest group was made up of traditional peaceful protesters participating in demonstrations sponsored by major labor and environmental groups like the AFL-CIO and the Sierra Club. But there were also small groups of protesters who hoped to engage in "direct action" to block the intersections between hotels where the WTO delegates were staying and the convention center where the meetings were held. These protests were to be "peaceful" in that there was to be no physical violence or property damage, but they did involve ignoring laws regulating pedestrian traffic. The smallest group was made up of self-styled anarchists who embraced tactics like randomly breaking windows of stores in the downtown area.

The actions of the second two varieties of protesters provoked a response by the Seattle police, who used rubber bullets and pepper spray in an attempt to open the blocked intersections and deter vandalism. The mayor of Seattle then declared a curfew and established a wide-ranging "no-protest" zone around the center of the city that barred all demonstrations, even peaceful demonstrations. The sometimes violent interactions between the protesters and the police produced a good deal of very dramatic film footage that was broadcast around the world describing what came known to be known as the "Battle in Seattle." Unfortunately, while property damage played a small part in the protests themselves, it was prominently displayed in media coverage.

Protesters later filed suit, claiming that the mayor's order and the police's actions had violated their First Amendment rights. The Ninth Circuit Court of Appeals later upheld the constitutionality of the city's actions[19] over the dissent of one judge who pointed out that the decision to deny admittance to the no-protest zone to anyone who expressed a political opinion while permitting shoppers and workers to enter the area unabated violated the city's constitutional duty to use the "least restrictive alternative" available.[20] He felt that the majority was making peaceful protesters pay for the excesses of a few lawbreakers.

The "Battle in Seattle" has had a profound effect on the way municipal authorities since then have responded to planned demonstrations at large conventions and meetings. Municipalities now appear to believe that any possibility of law breaking justifies wholesale curtailment of free speech rights of all demonstrators. This may well be a politically popular stance since local residents usually have little tolerance for protesters who inconvenience them as well as sully the good name of their hometown, but it ignores the question of whether the First Amendment permits such a draconian approach to dissent.

Unfortunately, the current official First Amendment enables this approach. We discussed in chapter 3 the Warren Court's crucial role in expanding the right of peaceful protest during the civil rights movement and the Vietnam War era. But the Burger, Rehnquist, and Roberts Courts have quietly dismantled the protections the Warren Court put in place. I will focus here on the Court's rulings on free speech use of what is called the "public forum"—streets, parks, and sidewalks. Here the post–Warren Supreme Court has articulated what appears at first glance to be a speech-friendly test, but it has then gone on to redefine the principal terms of the test to drastically narrow free speech protection. Let's first look at how the test reads and then study how it has been interpreted:

> In these quintessential public forums, the government may not prohibit all communicative activity. For the State to enforce a content-based exclusion it must show that its regulation is necessary to serve a compelling state interest and that it is narrowly drawn to achieve that end. The state may also enforce regulations of the time, place, and manner of expression which are content-neutral, are narrowly tailored to serve a significant government interest, and leave open ample alternative channels of communication.[21]

Let's decode this benign-sounding formula. First, we should recognize the impact of the rule's distinction between "content-based" and "content-neutral" laws. Content-based laws are hard to justify constitutionally, but content-neutral laws are permissible if they are "narrowly tailored" to achieve a "significant state interest" like traffic congestion. The problem here is that most laws are framed in content-neutral terms and the speech-repressive effect of such laws is just as great as that of content-discriminatory laws. So almost all laws municipalities pass will be judged by the less speech-protective rule despite their serious interference with free speech activities. The higher constitutional scrutiny reserved for content-based regulations seldom comes into play.

The protection afforded speech limited by content-neutral rules is diluted by the Court's new interpretation of the requirement that such laws be "narrowly tailored." As we saw in chapter 2, the Warren Court interpreted this requirement as mandating that the government use the means of achieving its goal that had the "least restrictive" effect on speech. If there were two effective means of promoting the state's goal, it had to use the method that had the lesser impact on speech. This speech-protective requirement was dramatically cut back in *Ward v. Rock v. Racism.*[22] *Ward* involved a rock concert promoting civil rights in New York's Central

Park. The organizers of the event challenged a municipal regulation that required the musicians to use not only a city-supplied sound system but also the services of city technicians who would even regulate the "mix" of different instruments so as to minimize noise. The federal district court ruled that the city regulation was not "narrowly tailored" since there were "less restrictive alternatives" for limiting noise, such as limits on overall decibel levels of the music. The Supreme Court disagreed, making clear that the "narrowly tailored" requirement now had a new meaning:

> [Lest] any confusion on the point remain, we re-affirm today that a regulation of the time, place, and manner of protected speech must be narrowly tailored to serve the government's legitimate content-neutral interests but that it need not be the least restrictive or least burdensome means of doing so. Rather [narrow] tailoring is satisfied so long as the regulation promotes a substantial government inter-est that would be achieved less effectively absent the regulation. [To] be sure this standard does not mean that a time, place, or manner regulation may burden substantially more speech than is necessary to further the government's legitimate interests.[23]

Narrow tailoring in the context of the facts of the *Ward* case now meant that the state only had to show that its anti-noise regulation would be more effective than no regulation at all. The new test used the same term as before, but completely changed its meaning.

The new rule for content-neutral regulations also requires that the regulation leave open "ample alternative channels of communication." But this requirement was also substantially diluted in *Heffron v. International Society for Krishna Consciousness.*[24] In that case, the Court ruled that the "ample alternative channels" requirement could easily be satisfied by pro-viding a special government-selected area for free speech activities even if the area was in a remote location. The case involved a rule at the Min-nesota State Fair that forbade the distribution of literature on the fair-grounds except from booths provided by the state. The Krishnas objected to this rule because the booths were in locations removed from the areas where most fair attendees traveled. The conservative majority upheld the rule on the ground that it was on its face content-neutral, served the state interest of preventing foot traffic congestion at the fair, and left open "ample alternative channels for communication" even though the govern-ment-assigned booths were remote from the main action.[25] It was the *Hef-*

fron case that inspired the "Demonstration Zones" later used by Boston to keep protesters far away from the areas where they might attract some media attention at the Democratic Convention in 2004. It might well also have inspired the Chinese Communist government to create its own "free speech zones" at the 2008 Olympics in Beijing.

The final nail in peaceful protest's coffin was driven in by the case of *Thomas v. Chicago Park District.*[26] The *Thomas* case concerned the procedures used by the Chicago Park District before granting a permit to use park property for a demonstration. The Warren Court had often used the prior-restraint doctrine to invalidate parade permit ordinances used by southern municipalities to suppress civil rights demonstrations like Martin Luther King Jr.'s march in Birmingham. These cases had held that permit systems that gave administrators broad discretion to deny a permit were prior restraints, thereby subjecting them to the highest First Amendment scrutiny. But in the *Thomas* case the conservative court held that a permit process with content-neutral time, place, and manner regulations was not a prior restraint so long as the justifications for denial were "reasonably specific and objective, and do not leave the decision to the whim of the administrator."[27] In fact, the regulations upheld in the *Thomas* case actually granted the administrator authority to deny a permit on a variety of both broad and vague grounds. For instance, a permit could be denied if "the use or activity intended by the applicant would present an unreasonable danger to the health or safety of the applicant, [users] of the park, [District] employees, or the public."[28]

Under the new constitutional regime, frustrating protest has become no more than an exercise in careful drafting. It is only necessary to set out a permit procedure that includes content-neutral regulations that use broad terms giving the administrator permission to strictly control marches or even deny a permit altogether while at the same time authorizing an alternative "demonstration zone" somewhere away from the action. The current Supreme Court's "public forum" rulings have enabled municipalities to make any protest unpleasant for the demonstrators and effective protest impossible. If the public officials in Montgomery and Birmingham and other sites of key civil rights demonstrations in the civil rights struggle had had the benefit of this interpretation of the First Amendment, they might well have been able to foil the attempts of Martin Luther King Jr. and the civil rights movement to end segregation.

I am suggesting that two of the major reasons why we see fewer public protests are that government officials would rather they did not occur and that the current official First Amendment does not adequately protect them. The two causes are not unrelated. I pointed out earlier that none of us is born a civil libertarian, and certainly municipal and police officials should be included in this psychological truism. We cannot expect them to grant activists more rights than the First Amendment requires. That is why it is so important that judges stand up for the right of all citizens to make their voices heard,. The "narrowly tailored" requirement was so important because it required local officials to infringe as little on free speech as possible. The present Supreme Court has effectively relieved them of that duty. I spoke in the introduction about the "official" and the "de facto" constitutions; the official Constitution is what the Supreme Court says the Constitution means; the de facto Constitution is what the government does when the Court is silent. But the distinction between the two concepts has begun to blur with regard to public demonstrations because the Supreme Court has adopted an interpretation that gives municipal officials full rein to do as they please.

This is a situation that could easily be remedied by the appointment of new justices to the Court who would reinstate the Warren Court rule. The new majority could reject the content-based/content-neutral approach and require that officials always apply the "least restrictive alternative" in limiting demonstrations. This term of art should be understood to mean that government can protect against harmful side effects of demonstrations but that the means chosen must respect free speech rights to the greatest degree practicable. It requires government to maximize speech opportunities as it attempts to minimize the unwanted consequences of public dissent. This requires a "balancing" of full free speech interests against the least expensive, most effective manner of limiting side effects. The decisions in particular cases will often be controversial, but controversial decisions are inevitable in constitutional law. At least the free speech interests will be considered by federal judges who are more sensitive to constitutional values than harried bureaucrats.

National Security Investigations

The First Amendment protects the right of association of activist groups because of the important role they play in the process of political change. They need access to the public forum to perform that function, but they also need protection from unwarranted governmental investigations that scare off potential supporters. Criminal investigations of activist organizations present a danger to democratic debate just as serious as laws curtailing peaceful political demonstrations, but the constitutional dimensions of investigations are more difficult to discuss. In contrast to laws limiting demonstrations that are public in nature, criminal investigations are secret, and we really never know of their existence until such time as the government files a criminal complaint and attempts to introduce the evidence gathered. If the government chooses not to file a criminal complaint, then these activities never become public and subject to judicial scrutiny. That's why in this chapter all I can do is summarize what we know now about the abuse of the investigatory power in the Vietnam era and point out that government officials in the post-9/11 era are subject to the same temptations to abuse power as were their predecessors. A second reason why the First Amendment dimensions of national security investigations are difficult to discuss is that the Supreme Court has refused to hear cases raising such issues on the grounds that the plaintiffs are not able to show sufficient injury to create an Article III "case" or "controversy." This deprives us of judicial discussions of the way investigations may interfere with conduct that the First Amendment (and other constitutional provisions) protects.

In one sense all nongovernmental groups attempting to affect policy decisions could be described as free speech activists. Activist groups include the Chamber of Commerce just as much as the ACLU, and even extend to corporate lobbyists. But I think that the First Amendment must show special solicitude for a subset of this larger group—activist groups that hold political views critical of government national security policy. These groups are more likely to attract the unwanted attention of government investigatory agencies and are less likely to be able to muster the political muscle to fight back without First Amendment support. Even a conservative like Justice Lewis K. Powell recognized the potential for government abuse: "History abundantly documents the tendency of government—however benevolent and benign its motives—to view with suspicion those who most fervently oppose its policies."[29] Recent history also documents that presidents, irrespective of party affiliation, have shown themselves willing to use all legal tools of their office (and sometimes even illegal ones) to neutralize such opposition on national security issues.

Rampant misuse of government investigatory powers on the grounds of national security took place during the civil rights and Vietnam War eras.[30] It started in the 1950s when the FBI instituted a secret program called COINTELPRO to disrupt the U.S. Communist Party by use of a variety of illegal techniques. The "national security" rationale that the FBI used to justify harassing the Communist Party was then stretched to justify the use of the same techniques against groups allegedly in danger of infiltration by Communist agents. This line of reasoning led to the FBI's investigation of the NAACP and its decade-long attempt to destroy Martin Luther King Jr. as a political leader. When political opposition to the Vietnam War arose, COINTELPRO again was expanded to target antiwar groups like the Students for a Democratic Society (SDS) on the grounds that their "unpatriotic" conduct could only be explained by Communist infiltration. The ambit of government investigations eventually expanded so that by the late sixties and early seventies almost every major group active in attempts to bring about political change in war or civil rights policy found itself a target of government surveillance.[31]

The size of the government surveillance programs during the sixties and seventies shocks us today. Here is a brief summary. The FBI opened almost 500,000 "subversive" files and another 30,000 files investigating "extremism." Between 1955 and 1975 it conducted 740,000 "subversive" investigations and almost 200,000 "extremism" investigations. And the FBI was not alone. The army had its own domestic intelligence surveillance program that opened files on 100,000 opponents of the war, including prominent citizens and members of Congress. The army disseminated the material it collected, including information on the private political, financial, and sex lives of tens of thousands of citizens, to local police, the FBI, the CIA, and the National Security Agency (NSA). The CIA also instituted an illegal intelligence program on domestic dissidents—called CHAOS—that compiled intelligence on critics of the war, ultimately accumulating data on 300,000 people that it too shared with the White House and other agencies. Even The IRS followed suit by targeting 10,000 individuals for tax investigations because of their political activities. And we should also remember that the NSA, so active in spying on American citizens today, obtained copies of millions of telegrams sent between 1947 and 1975 from which it created a "watch list" of suspect individuals and organizations.

The federal government was not alone in the national security investigation business; local and state governments operated their own internal "intelligence" units that had a long history of harassing leftist groups and individuals they labeled "radicals," "agitators," and "subversives."[32] And these local intelligence operations did not lack for resources. In Chicago, for instance, the police department's Security Section had as many as five hundred officers in 1968. The total number of federal, state, and local undercover agents working subversive investigations in Chicago was over one thousand. Other major American cities had similar intelligence operations, and these local intelligence units shared the information they collected with each other and with federal and state authorities.

These "national security" investigations often lasted long after the alleged national security justification had been disproved. For instance, the agents originally assigned to conduct the FBI investigation of the NAACP on the grounds that it might be a target of Communist infiltration quickly discovered that no such infiltration existed, but the investigation itself continued for another twenty years. By the late sixties, even the pretext of a national security or criminal link was discarded, and officials routinely authorized investigations of any activist group that opposed government policy.

We should also remember the wide variety of techniques, some blatantly illegal, that were used in these investigations. Press-clippings files were kept and undercover agents sent to public meetings of the target groups. Aggressive "fact-finding" interviews were used to warn individuals of the danger of further involvement with certain groups. Agents infiltrated the leadership of target groups, a tactic that permitted the informant to eavesdrop and report on confidential conversations. But some informants went even further to influence the groups' actions, sometimes even urging illegal action. Government investigators also made surreptitious entries to steal mail, plant "bugs," and wiretap telephone calls without obtaining a warrant.

All these actions were kept secret from the public and the courts. We only know about them now because the public uproar over the Watergate scandal motivated the Senate to set up a special committee chaired by Senator Frank Church to investigate government surveillance practices during Vietnam; the Church Committee authored a multivolume report documenting the abuses. The Church Committee discovered that these investigations often went beyond merely collecting information on dissidents; often the government agencies took actions to harass and disrupt the First Amendment– protected activities of target groups. As the Church Committee report stated, the government aim was no less than to "deter citizens from joining groups, 'neutralize' those who were already members, and prevent or inhibit the expression of ideas."[33]

A 1968 internal FBI memo to field offices quoted in the Church Committee report provides a good summary of the tactics authorized for use against "New Left" groups like SDS. Agents were instructed to prepare leaflets using the "most obnoxious pictures" of New Left leaders, to instigate "personal conflicts or animosities" within the target organizations, to create the impression that the leaders were "informants for the Bureau or other law enforcement agencies," to send articles from student newspapers showing the "depravity" of New Left leaders to university officials, donors, legislators, and parents, to arrest group members on marijuana charges, to send anonymous letters to students' parents and their employers about their activities, to plant negative stories about the target organizations with "cooperative press contacts," and to use "misinformation" to "confuse and disrupt" New Left activities by notifying members that events had been canceled.[34]

One cannot help but wonder how successful these government attempts to "neutralize" opposition groups were. We do know that antiwar activist groups like the SDS were manifestly less effective in the years after 1968 when the government programs were at their peak. One can only speculate to what extent these groups self-destructed and to what extent they were victims of a successful government campaign of "dirty tricks." The fact that the government officials allocated so many resources to these programs over so many years suggests that they thought the operations were effective. And just as we do not know what effect these tactics had on the individuals and groups targeted, so we also do not know how many citizens chose not to actively oppose the war because they feared that participation would attract the unwanted attention of government investigators. The most prudent course of action is often inaction, but this type of government-induced political passivity also undermines the foundations of democratic government.

The government's secret abuse of its investigatory powers became public after Watergate, and in response to the public outrage Congress and the executive branch instituted reforms to ensure that this history would not repeat itself. Unfortunately, these are the very reforms that have been methodically dismantled since 9/11 on grounds of national security. Government secrecy prevents us from knowing much about how the government is using its powers of investigation today, but we do know that it now has amassed an enormous arsenal of investigative techniques that it can use. At the very least, the existence of this arsenal chills political activity; at worst it enables a repeat of the Vietnam-era abuses.

Take the investigatory powers of the FBI as an example. There were legislative proposals to prevent FBI abuse of its investigatory powers, but unfortunately they were never passed. Instead, the reform took the form of internal guidelines issued by President Gerald Ford's attorney general, Edward Levi. These guidelines were well received by civil libertarians because they insisted that any investigation must be triggered by some indication that the target had engaged or planned to engage in criminal conduct. A citizen who had done nothing to indicate violation of a law was not to be a target of the investigatory powers of the federal government. But internal Justice Department guidelines, unlike legislation, can be repealed by the stroke of the next attorney general's pen. And later attorney generals have constantly whittled down the protections Levi put in place. George W. Bush's first attorney general, John Ashcroft, finally removed the need for evidence of criminal activity before instigating government surveillance for antiterrorism assessments.[35] Now the FBI can open a file on a citizen in the United States without individual suspicion if it relates to a national security assessment. In conducting the assessment, agents can employ informants, engage in physical surveillance, and conduct interviews without identifying themselves as federal agents. An agent can also surf the internet and search government databases as well as utilize commercial firms that collect and collate private information on individuals from a large variety of sources.

Congress has added to the potential for abuse by authorizing the issuance of a "national security letter" (NSL).[36] These are administrative subpoenas issued without judicial approval. NSLs require credit card companies, banks, telephone companies, and internet providers to disclose private information about individuals even when there is no individualized suspicion of criminal wrongdoing. There is no need to notify the individual or group of this invasion of its privacy. And the request need not be limited to information on one individual; for instance, an internet provider's entire database could be the subject of such a request so long as the contents of individual emails were not divulged. National security letters can be used like a giant informational vacuum cleaner.

Another powerful investigatory tool is the FISA warrant. Traditionally, courts have only authorized wiretaps and other invasive investigative techniques after the government has made a showing of probable cause of criminal conduct. But Congress in the late seventies passed the Foreign Intelligence Surveillance Act (FISA),[37] which authorized the issuance of special warrants based on a weaker burden of proof for foreign intelligence investigations. These FISA warrants are issued by a special court located in Washington, D.C. The goal of the FISA legislation was to give the executive branch some leeway in foreign intelligence investigations while preserving the probable-cause requirement for domestic investigations, but the Patriot Act extended the use of FISA warrants to domestic cases so long as a "significant purpose" of the interception was the pursuit of foreign intelligence. This new authority allows the government to end run the "probable cause" requirement that should be required for warrants on cases targeting domestic dissent, making possible the same abuse of investigatory powers that FISA was intended to remedy. And the FISA court has shown itself to be quite generous in granting government requests for FISA warrants. Almost no FISA requests have been denied. Not only have the authorizations been numerous, but they have also been very broad in scope, permitting government eavesdropping on computers, faxes, land and cell phones, and emails.[38]

But the Bush administration found even broad FISA authority to be inadequate for its purposes. The *New York Times* (on the basis of one of those unauthorized leaks discussed in chapter 4) reported that the National Security Agency (NSA) was intercepting the email messages of U.S. citizens on American soil without the authority of a FISA warrant. This secret program appeared to be a blatant violation of the FISA statute as well as the First and Fourth Amendments, but the Bush administration defended it as a proper exercise of the president's powers as commander-in-chief as envisaged by the National Security Presidency discussed in chapter 1. Congress later passed legislation approving the program, and courts have refused to rule on its constitutionality on the grounds that plaintiffs challenging it do not have the requisite standing. This refusal has enabled the government to operate the program in complete secrecy, so we do not know exactly who are the targets of these warrantless investigations, but in light of NSA's participation in the Vietnam-era abuses, there is no reason not to believe that free speech activists are on the list. Journalists and human rights lawyers interviewing or representing anti-government groups in the Middle East would seem to have every reason to suspect that their communications with their sources or their clients are being monitored by the NSA.

Not only has the executive branch and Congress made it much easier for the government to collect information on American citizens, but they have also insisted that the information generated be given the widest possible distribution. In the name of national security the "fire walls" between various federal agencies like the FBI and CIA have been taken down and the federal government has also entered into information-sharing agreements with local and state police intelligence units. On one scale, this is all to the good; information sharing should result in more efficient law enforcement. But it also multiplies the chances for mistake or abuse. All the information gathered by federal, state, and local agencies is then centralized in federal government databases open to all these various law enforcement organizations. A necessary consequence of this information sharing is that more law enforcement agencies, many with abysmal records on respecting civil liberties, now have access to enormous amounts of private information on American citizens. And the potential for abuse is only expanded by sophisticated computer programs that government uses to sift through the mountains of data it collects to uncover "links" and "patterns" of allegedly suspicious activity.[39]

All Americans have reason to worry about their government creating dossiers on law-abiding citizens, but most of us can take some comfort in numbers. There are so many citizens and so much information involved that it is unlikely that any one individual will become the target of a government investigation. The programs' enormous scope works against their threat to the privacy of any individual. But of course, this safeguard does not extend to free speech activists. They are the citizens who are taking actions that will attract the government's attention. Consider the plight of a hypothetical first-year law student considering engaging in any of a variety of First Amendment–protected activities. He or she might be thinking of joining an organization opposing U.S. policy in the Middle East, making a contribution to the legal defense fund of an Arab-American nationalist, or attending a rally against America's inaction on the issue of global warning. Each of these actions now carries the risk of attracting the attention of federal, state, or local investigatory agencies. And if the student's name is recorded by any of these agencies, it will become part of a huge network of databases that a large number of other government agencies can access. Once the information is in the system, it will not be corrected because of the need for secrecy. There is no way the student can know what agencies or organizations will, legally or illegally, have access to this information. Might it come into the hands of the state agency that licenses new lawyers? Might it be leaked to potential employers? There is no end of ways that this record of what the government has deemed suspicious activity might come back to haunt the student. Once again the prudent course might be to refrain from any action that might attract attention.

There is some anecdotal evidence of the government abusing its investigatory powers since 9/11. One example is a report issued by the ACLU of Northern California on government surveillance of political groups in northern and central California.[40] The report documented several different agencies using a variety of techniques to keep tabs on groups involved in protected free speech activities. The groups ranged from anti–Iraq War activists to animal rights and women's rights groups. The ACLU report only disclosed abuses that inadvertently became public in one geographic area. We just do not know whether this is the tip of the iceberg.

We should not take too much comfort in the fact that there is no evidence of misuse of the information collected on activists since 9/11. The abuses of the Vietnam era only became public long after they occurred. And it is clear that in related areas—like interrogation of terrorist suspects—the Bush administration prided itself on pushing its legal powers to their outermost limits (and sometimes beyond) in its efforts to combat terrorism.[41] And we have every right to take with a grain of salt the statements of high-level officials that they always follow the letter of the law regarding investigations. Not only are the laws and regulations that exist very permissive, but we saw in chapter 2 that officials sometimes feel entitled to dissemble where national security interests are involved. But even if there were no violation of statutory or constitutional rights, the damage to political activism would still be substantial because the very existence of these wide-ranging powers transmits a clear message: The government is watching you. And the agencies watching are the very organs of government that have authority to initiate prosecutions There will, of course, always be activists who accept these risks, but what we really need is a politics that welcomes the involvement of all our citizens, not just the brazen. In fact, we especially need the participation of more ordinary citizens.

Protecting Political Activists

What we need now is a First Amendment that recognizes that government investigations of political activists raise issues of a constitutional dimension. In cases like *NAACP v. Alabama* [42] and *Shelton v. Tucker*[43] the Warren Court established that the First Amendment protects the privacy of political activists against government demands for confidential information. That principle of organizational privacy should apply no less when the government uses its investigatory powers to obtain that same information. The Burger Court had an opportunity to apply freedom of association privacy principles to government investigations in the 1972 case of *Laird v. Tatum*.[44] Unfortunately, the newly created conservative majority refused to rule on the First Amendment issue, ruling instead that the plaintiffs in the case did not have requisite standing to bring the lawsuit. We will return to the Supreme Court's misuse of the standing doctrine in chapter 6. What we need now is a Supreme Court that will interpret the First Amendment to apply to government investigations. This would not mean that activist groups would be immune from government investigations, but it would mean that government agencies would have to show some indication of criminal wrongdoing before drawing citizens' groups into its investigatory web.

Once the Supreme Court has articulated the constitutional principles, it makes sense for Congress to pass legislation implementing those principles into a larger system that courts can monitor. It was a mistake for Congress not to legislate reforms of national security investigations after Watergate. We should not expect the executive branch to adequately police itself in this area. A congressional statute should set out the constitutional parameters for investigations as the Freedom of Information Act (FOIA) sets out the parameters for citizen access to government information. This charter should reflect not only First Amendment values but also Fourth Amendment and due process principles. Such a statute would give clear guidance to investigatory agencies like the FBI as to what they can and cannot do and would provide standards for federal judges to enforce.

All I can do here is set out some of the necessary principles. The most important principle such legislation should announce is that no investigatory activity should be commenced against a citizen or group unless there is an indication of past or future commission of a federal crime. The insistence that the government leave law-abiding citizens alone is one of those basic standards that separate democracies from totalitarian states. Requiring that the initiation of government investigations be linked to past or future criminal conduct will not hamper efforts to stop terrorist violence since these efforts inevitably involve breaking laws. The FBI did not lack authority to investigate the terrorists responsible for the 9/11 attacks; the terrorists had overstayed their visas in violation of federal law and had engaged in activity indicating possible future crimes. The FBI had sufficient legal authority; it just failed to follow up on available leads.

The statute should also set out a list of approved investigative techniques and the factual showing necessary to justify the use of each. The most invasive techniques should only be employed after less invasive techniques have been found ineffectual. The most serious invasions, like bugging, wiretapping, and the use of undercover agents for purposes of infiltration, should require an order from a federal district court.

Citizens should also be made aware of the fact that they are targets of investigations. Temporary secrecy may sometimes be necessary, but at some point citizens must be notified that they are the subjects of government surveillance so that they can clear up honest misunderstandings or challenge illegal governmental activity. Agencies should also be required to keep records that will enable citizens to bring suit for misconduct, including the award of damages and attorney fees in appropriate cases. The most effective way to deter government abuse of its powers is to hold the government responsible for its illegal conduct.

6

The Supreme Court

It is emphatically the province and the duty of the judicial department to say what the law is.
　　　　　　　　　　　　　—Chief Justice John Marshall

The failure of the Supreme Court to interpret the First Amendment in a way that adequately supports democratic debate has been a recurring theme of this book. This chapter concentrates on two other failures of the Supreme Court to fulfill its duty to (in John Marshall's words) "say what the law is."[1] The first is the Court's refusal to clearly reject the National Security Presidency's claim that the president has independent power to initiate the use of military force. Instead, the Court has adopted a vague formula that in practice condones the president's independent use of force. The second failure is the Court's use of the technical doctrine of standing to prevent courts from ruling on cases raising important statutory and constitutional issues. This failure immunizes executive law breaking from judicial inquiry.

Preempting Debate

We saw in chapter 1 that President Bush argued that the president must have the discretion to act in the area of national security without congressional authorization, and even in the face of congressional opposition. And while President Obama has spoken in more moderate tones, he has not rejected an expansive conception of presidential power over national security. Critics often blame Congress for acquiescing in this executive power grab, and the criticism is a just one. But I want to point to another constitutional villain—the United States Supreme Court. The Court has had opportunities to reject the National Security Presidency's views on independent presidential power but has passed them over. Instead, it prefers to articulate a vague constitutional formula that for the most part gives presidents full rein to do what they please in the area of national security.

I wish to concentrate on the issue of whether the president has independent power to initiate offensive military operations without congressional consent. This is usually discussed as an issue of separation of powers, but I wish to emphasize its free speech dimensions. The First Amendment empowers individuals and groups to have their voices heard at all levels before government officials act. If they are able to marshal opposition to a presidential proposal to initiate combat, they can deny him the authority to initiate combat that may evolve into a long war. But this democratic control disappears if the president acts without the consent of Congress, or even fails to notify them in advance of his military plans. His independent decision not only preempts prior debate about the wisdom of the particular action in question but also prejudices later debates by creating a new reality that opponents must accept as the status quo. The president's policies are no longer proposals but concrete "facts on the ground" that all future discussions must take into account. It is no longer a question of whether we should do x, but rather of what we should do now that we have done x. And while critics are debating that question, the president can independently act once again to create an even newer reality. Debate is never able to catch up to the events it is intended to shape.[2]

A hypothetical might help to show how this political scenario works. In 2008 there was a steady drumbeat of announcements from the George W. Bush White House that Iran was attempting to build the capacity to construct nuclear weapons, that for Iran to hold those weapons endangered American national security, and that "all options were on the table" to prevent such an occurrence. The administration hinted that bombing suspected nuclear sites in Iran was one such option and, according to many sources, was actually the option preferred by President Bush and Vice-President Cheney. No one suggested that President Bush needed congressional authorization for such bombings; President Bush would do it under his power as commander-in-chief.

Bombing Iran would be an act of war and might well produce disastrous results for the world in general and the United States in particular. At the very least, Iran would hold its oil off the world market, and it might also sabotage oil production efforts in other oil-producing states like

Saudi Arabia, thereby further escalating the price of oil. It could also use its military forces to attack U.S. troops in Iraq and Afghanistan, complicating further the difficult American military involvement in those areas. Of course, we could also sketch out more optimistic scenarios. Iran might succumb to American threats of bombing before the bombing took place, or perhaps the bombing might incite a popular overthrow of the Iranian government. The point I wish to stress is that the bombing would dramatically change the terms of debate. If the bombing had been ordered, and the more pessimistic scenario had unrolled, critics would in one sense have been proven correct, but such vindication would be to a large extent irrelevant because the bombing would have created a new reality and the pressing political issue then would no longer be the wisdom of a war against Iran but the best way to win it.

This would mean that the president would have engaged the United States in a serious war without congressional authorization. This certainly is not the decision-making procedure for initiating combat that the authors of the Constitution envisaged. Listen to the comments of one of the framers, James Wilson, on this point: "This system will not hurry us into war; it is calculated to guard against it. It will not be in the power of a single man, or a single body of men, to involve us in such distress. . . ."[3] Nor is it the procedure that presidents followed for the first 160 years of our history. But since the second half of the twentieth century American presidents of both parties have claimed more and more unilateral power. We are all aware of Congress's feeble attempts to stop the erosion of its Article I powers, but we also need to emphasize the role the U.S. Supreme Court has played in condoning this constitutional takeover by the presidency.

The Youngstown Case

The Supreme Court case most relevant to presidential claims of unilateral power in the national security area is *Youngstown Sheet & Tube v. Sawyer.*[4] We talked about *Youngstown* in chapter 1, but now I would like to spend more time explaining its importance to the constitutional war over national security. In 1952 President Truman seized privately owned steel mills in order to forestall a strike he feared would interrupt the production of steel necessary for the Korean war effort. Since Congress had recently considered and rejected granting the president power to seize private property during labor disputes, Truman relied primarily on his claim of independent power to act without congressional authorization. The Supreme Court held the seizure to be beyond the president's powers, but the various members of the majority articulated different theories to justify their votes. And these different theories pointed in different directions for the future of presidential power in the area of foreign affairs.

Justice Black wrote the majority opinion. He rejected all the president's claims to independent power. For Black, neither the "vesting" clause of Article II ("the executive power shall be vested in a president") nor the commander-in-chief power, either alone or together, gave the president the power to act without congressional authorization. Black argued that the constitutional text made clear that Congress would make the basic legislative decisions and the president's authority and duty were limited to executing the policies Congress chose. The president's only role in the law-making process was "the recommending of laws he thought wise and vetoing laws he thought bad."[5]

Although Black's was the majority opinion, Justice Jackson's concurring opinion has proved to be more influential in setting the framework for analyzing later uses of presidential power. Instead of Black's insistence that the president must point to legislation granting him authority to act, Jackson (who as FDR's attorney general had written legal opinions justifying Roosevelt's expansive use of presidential power before World War II) painted a more fluid picture of the relationship between the president and Congress.

Jackson proposed three different situations for the exercise of presidential power on issues concerning foreign affairs: (1) when the president acted with the agreement of Congress, (2) when he acted in defiance of congressional legislation, and (3) and when he acted in situations in which Congress took no position pro or con. It was in this last context that Jackson felt the fluidity is to be the greatest. Here the president must

> rely on his own independent powers, but there is a zone of twilight in which he and Congress might have concurrent authority, or in which its distribution is uncertain. Therefore, congressional inertia, indifference or quiescence may sometimes, at least as a practical matter, enable, if not invite, measures on independent presidential responsibility. In this area, any actual test of power is likely to depend on the imperatives of events and contemporary imponderables rather than on abstract theories of law.[6]

The phrase "enable, if not invite" is an odd one to see in a legal opinion supposedly setting out the boundaries of executive power. Its attempt to avoid rigidity resulted in an ambiguity that the executive branch has been able to use to expand its independent powers exponentially. And Justice Frankfurter's concurrence also placed its own pro- executive spin on Jackson's twilight zone of congressional silence:

> In short, a systematic, unbroken, executive practice, long pursued to the knowledge of the Congress and never before questioned, engaged in by Presidents who have also sworn to uphold the Constitution, making as it were such exercise of power a part of the structure of our government, may be treated as a gloss on "executive power" vested in the president.[7]

Both Jackson and Frankfurter ruled that Congress had denied the president the power that Truman claimed in *Youngstown,* so their comments about the twilight zone are only dicta not binding on later courts. But the Rehnquist Court later explicitly made the move that Jackson and Frankfurter had only hinted at. In *Dames & Moore v. Regan,*[8] Chief Justice Rehnquist (who had clerked for Justice Jackson the year *Youngstown* was decided) relied on both the Jackson and Frankfurter concurrences to craft his own version of the twilight zone. Rehnquist's majority opinion for the first time held that where there is no congressional grant of authority to the president to act on certain issues, a history of congressional acquiescence in the exercise of presidential power raises a presumption that the president's actions were taken with congressional consent.[9] In such cases silence equals consent, and fact patterns that at first glance might seem to fit into Jackson's classification of congressional silence are transformed into cases of congressional approval.

This subtle change in constitutional doctrine has created a dramatic shift in the power balance between Congress and the president. Not only is it based on a very questionable logical premise—that somehow one branch's failure to act expands the power of another branch—but in practice it concedes to the president independent powers the Constitution never intended to give him. Now presidential power can be premised on Congress's failure to pass legislation. The only way to clearly deny him power is to pass legislation negating such a grant, but, as Harold Koh has pointed out,[10] it is extremely difficult for Congress to explicitly deny the president power in the area of foreign affairs. The reasons should be clear to readers of the first five chapters of this book. The president has unrivaled access to the media, and he controls the flow of most information relating to national security, a fact that gives his views a special persuasiveness in a national security–related debate. So, too, he is the leader of one of the two major political parties, and members of his own party are reluctant to ever refuse him their support, especially on national security issues.

And even passing a law denying the president the power to bomb without authorization would not suffice to rebut the presumption of approval in *Dames & Moore* unless it survived a presidential veto.[11] If vetoed, the law would have to be repassed by a two-thirds majority of both houses of Congress.

Let's apply the Jackson/Frankfurter/Rehnquist approach to the hypothetical bombing of Iran. Since, as I will detail later in this chapter, there is a history in recent years of presidents unilaterally ordering military actions against unfriendly regimes, the president could point to a history of congressional acquiescence in such actions that would raise the presumption of consent that Chief Justice Rehnquist set out in *Dames & Moore v. Regan.* Therefore, congressional silence might well be considered approval. Therefore, Congress would have had to pass a joint resolution over President Bush's veto denying the president that power, a well-nigh impossible feat.[12]

But the Jackson concurrence does more than tip the scales towards finding congressional approval of presidential actions in the national security area; it also recognizes that he has "his own independent powers" to act without congressional approval. And the Supreme Court since *Youngstown* has refused to define what these independent presidential powers are, a refusal that has permitted presidents to define them. The Court has made it a practice not to rule on presidential claims of independent power, preferring instead to pass over these controversial claims to decide cases on other, less controversial grounds. This allows these expansive claims of presidential autonomy to operate as our de facto Constitution in all situations that do not reach the Court.

Consider the 2004 Supreme Court case of *Hamdi v. Rumsfeld*,[13] a case that involved the legality of a Bush executive order that authorized the government to imprison a U.S. citizen on U.S. soil indefinitely as an "enemy combatant." When the legality of the detention was challenged as beyond the president's power, Bush's first argument was that Article II gave him the power to set up the program under his own independent authority. His claim was analogous to that which President Truman had claimed and Justice Black had rejected in *Youngstown*. Justice O'Conner's opinion neither accepted nor rejected the president's controversial assertion. Instead, she upheld the president's power under situation (1) of the formula set out in Jackson's concurrence; here was a case where Congress had approved the presidential detention program under a broad grant of authority called the Authorization for Use of Military Force (AUMF), which Congress had passed soon after the 9/11 attacks. "We do not reach the question of whether Article II provides such authority . . . because we agree with the Government's alternative position, that Congress has authorized the detention through the AUMF."[14] The AUMF did not mention detaining suspects indefinitely without trial as the Bush order permitted, but it did authorize the president to use "all necessary and appropriate force" against "nations, organizations, and persons associated with the September 11, 1991 terrorist attacks."[15] The Court found that this vague provision authorized the detaining of enemy combatants. Perhaps Justice O'Connor felt she had cleverly avoided ruling on the controversial issue of independent presidential power, but in fact she had, by refusing to reject his claim to independent power, enabled him and other presidents to rely on that power in other situations.[16] She had failed to fulfill the Court's duty to "say what the law is."

Another important case bearing on the president's national security powers, *Hamdan v. Rumsfeld*,[17] reached the Court in 2006. It involved the military commissions President Bush had established after 9/11 to try noncitizens who either were members of al-Qaeda or were suspected of engaging in terrorist activities against the United States. The plaintiff was a Yemeni citizen who had acted as Osama bin Laden's driver. Hamdan, who had been captured in Afghanistan and held at Guantanamo, challenged the legality of such a military commission to try him. Once again the president claimed he had independent authority to set up the commissions without congressional approval. Like Justice O'Connor in *Hamdi*, Justice Stevens refused to rule on this claim. Instead, he relied on Justice Jackson's *Youngstown* concurrence to rule that this was a situation in which the Congress had authorized commissions subject to certain limitations that the president's program ignored. "Whether or not the president has independent powers, absent congressional authorization, to convene military commissions, he may not disregard limits that Congress has, in the proper exercise of its powers, placed on his powers. *Youngstown Sheet & Tube Co. v. Sawyer*, . . . (Jackson, J. concurring)."[18]

The Bush administration was therefore forced to argue that Congress had in fact authorized Bush to set up the challenged commissions without the alleged limitations. Bush's lawyers relied on several congressional statutes, including the same AUMF that had been interpreted in *Hamdi* to constitute congressional authorization for detaining enemy combatants. Their argument had some logical force since the commissions, like the "enemy combatant" program approved in *Hamdi,* were part of the administration's response to 9/11. But this time the Court refused to give the AUMF a broad interpretation because such an interpretation would conflict with provisions in the Uniform Code of Military Justice (UCMJ). "[T]here is nothing in the text or legislative history of the AUMF that even hints that Congress intended to expand or alter the authorization set forth in Article 21 of the UCMJ."[19] Stevens concluded that the military commissions fit, like Truman's seizure of the steel mills in *Youngstown,* into Jackson's second category of presidents acting in violation of congressional legislation.[20]

Commentators saw both *Hamdi* and *Hamdan* as major repudiations of the Bush administration's theory of presidential powers. In one way the commentators were correct since *Hamdi* held that even congressionally approved presidential orders must provide for constitutional rights like due process of law, and *Hamdan* held that the president must comply with congressional limits on his power. But in another important sense, these cases were a victory for the National Security Presidency because the Court had refused to reject the Bush administration's theory of independent presidential power. Since the Court has not said that this is an erroneous interpretation of the Constitution, the president is able to continue to operate under this controversial constitutional premise in all those instances where the Court does not rule that Congress has denied him the power.

When we review our history over the last sixty years, we see that presidents have made good use of the Court's silence to reset the constitutional balance on issues of war and peace in their favor. Time and again, we see the same scenario play out. The president orders the American military to take offensive action without congressional consent, citing his own authority as commander-in-chief. Sometimes he notifies congressional leaders just before the act and/or makes mention of some existing statute that allegedly authorizes it. For instance, in 1950 (even before the *Youngstown* case) President Truman ordered American troops without congressional authorization into South Korea to repel an invasion by

North Korean forces, thereby engaging the United States in a major land war in Asia. In 1961, President Kennedy similarly independently authorized an invasion of Cuba by an army of Cuban exiles trained and directed by the CIA. This led to the Bay of Pigs fiasco. In 1965 President Johnson on his own authority ordered American troops into the Dominican Republic, allegedly to protect the lives of American citizens but actually to prevent a leftist takeover. Later Johnson also autonomously authorized a secret war against leftist rebels in Laos; that war lasted nine years. In 1969, President Nixon ordered secret bombing raids of the neutral country of Cambodia. In 1983, President Reagan ordered an invasion of the island of Grenada, again allegedly to protect American medical students but in truth to install a government more favorable to American interests.

We must remember that this has been a policy of both Democratic and Republican presidents. Not only did Presidents Truman, Kennedy, and Johnson authorize military action on their own authority, but so did President Clinton. In 1998, Clinton on his own authority ordered cruise missile strikes against alleged hideouts of Osama bin Laden in the Sudan and Afghanistan in reprisal for attacks on American embassies in Africa. And in 1999, Clinton, without congressional authorization, ordered American planes to lead a major NATO bombing campaign against the Serbian-controlled government of Yugoslavia in response to human rights abuses in Kosovo.

It is true that sometimes presidents have felt it in their political interests to obtain congressional authorization for military action. President Johnson asked for the Gulf of Tonkin Resolution before committing major combat forces to Vietnam. The first President Bush obtained congressional authorization for the first Gulf War, and the second President Bush also got approval for the later invasions of Afghanistan and Iraq. But even in these cases, the president accepted the congressional support while making clear that he was not constitutionally required to obtain it before acting pursuant to his own independent powers.

In the introduction, we distinguished between "official" and "challenger" interpretations of the Constitution. The official Constitution is what the courts say; the challenger hopes to replace it. But we also mentioned a third category: the de facto Constitution. The de facto Constitution is the one that actually operates in practice when courts are silent. We might say now that the Jackson concurrence serves as our "official" text of presidential national security powers, and the National Security

Presidency is its challenger. But in cases where Congress has not acted to limit presidential power, the National Security Presidency also operates as the de facto Constitution. To the extent that the National Security Presidency argues that the president's commander-in-chief powers prevail over specific congressional legislation, the *Hamdan* case clearly rejects it. But with regard to the principle that the president can act independently where Congress is silent, the official Constitution is ambiguous, and the de facto Constitution recognizes that power. This means in effect that the president can order the use of American military force at will. We should not be surprised that President Bush believed he had the authority to bomb Iran.

The Myth of Independent Presidential Power

No one doubts that the president needs broad power in the area of foreign affairs, and that our Constitution gives him such power. His Article II authority gives him the leading role in establishing our foreign policy and enables him to direct the enormous federal bureaucracy in achieving his foreign policy goals. He also has constitutional power to negotiate treaties, subject to the Senate power to approve them. When those powers are not enough, Article II also directs him to recommend to Congress "measures he judges necessary and expedient." And the powers of presidential speech ensure that Congress usually accepts his advice. Not only can the president recommend laws he likes; he can veto those he does not. And once Congress has authorized military action, the president as commander-in-chief of the armed forces has authority to manage the actions Congress authorizes.

Of course, there is always the problem of presidential power to act in an emergency before Congress can meet. The authors of the Constitution were aware of this problem. From the outset they assumed that the commander-in-chief power included power to "repel sudden attacks."[21] But this was clearly a defensive power to be used until such time as Congress could act. And when the president does act defensively without congressional authorization, our constitutional tradition is clear that he should inform the Congress as soon as possible and ask them to ratify his actions. This gives the president power to act in an emergency but does not invite him to act extralegally except in the direst circumstances. He has reason to be cautious in his acts because there is no guarantee that Congress will ratify them. They might choose to impeach him instead.

What our Constitution does not do is grant the president independent authority to initiate offensive military action. It is clear that the Constitution's authors intended for the power to initiate wars to reside in the Congress. And they had good reason for this allocation of powers. Too often under the British system of separation of powers, they had seen the king initiate wars that the taxpayers paid for and in which the commoners died. They wanted the overlapping constituencies that the Senate, the House of Representatives, and the presidency represent to be in accord before military steps are taken that cannot later be undone. This constitutional policy judgment looks just as wise in the twenty-first century as it did in the eighteenth.

Justice Black's majority opinion in *Youngstown* had it right. Black's majority opinion clearly denied the president independent power while Jackson's concurrence assumed he had some undefined modicum of independent power. By adopting the Jackson approach, the current Supreme Court has enabled the president to authorize offensive military action at will.

The Supreme Court should clearly state that the president only has power to initiate military actions (other than repelling enemy attacks) that Congress authorizes. This clear statement of a constitutional rule would encourage the president to involve the Congress in his deliberations, just as the vague wording of the Jackson concurrence invites him to ignore Congress. Of course, there will always be grey areas where the president's independent foreign affairs powers blend into Congress's power to authorize military action. The answer here is not a vague formula that dodges the crucial question but the passage by Congress of legislation that provides a process for handling the close calls. Admittedly, Congress's last attempt to pass such legislation—the War Powers Resolution—has been a failure. But the Supreme Court should take part of the blame for this failure. Its refusal to reject the theory of independent presidential power has given presidents an excuse to ignore the War Power Resolution as an unconstitutional infringement on the president's powers. If the Supreme Court would make clear that the president needs the Congress's consent to initiate military action, he would have an incentive to cooperate with Congress to provide a workable process that respects the role of both branches of government.

Standing

So far I have argued that the Supreme Court has failed in its duty to say what the law is by adopting vague formulas that do not resolve important issues like independent presidential power. Another way the Court can fail its duty is by refusing to accept a case at all. The Court can refuse to hear a case challenging government conduct on the grounds that the plaintiff does not have the "standing" necessary to constitute a "case" or a "controversy" as required by Article III. Until the late 1970s, the Supreme Court had only required plaintiffs to show a personal stake in the outcome of the litigation sufficient to ensure that they would vigorously present their side of the case,[22] but the Burger, Rehnquist, and Roberts Courts have transformed the standing requirement into an obstacle course for citizens challenging the legality of government conduct. It started in 1974 with the case of *United States v. Richardson;*[23] the plaintiffs in that case were taxpayers who argued that Article I's mandate that "a regular Statement of Account of the Receipts and Expenditures of all public Money shall be published from time to time" applied to expenditures made by the CIA. As taxpayers, they wanted to know how their money was being spent. This lawsuit reflected the tension we discussed in chapter 4 between the need of citizens to know what their government is doing and the competing need for secrecy in some contexts. But instead of wrestling with this important constitutional issue, Chief Justice Burger's opinion dismissed the lawsuit because the plaintiffs did not have "standing" to bring it before the Court. They may have had a "genuine interest in the use of the funds," but they could not claim the "particular concrete injury" the Court now required.[24] Since then, the conservative majority has dismissed a variety of lawsuits challenging the legality of executive conduct on this technical ground.[25] The consequence of such a negative ruling is that government can continue its preferred course of conduct, even if it violates congressional law or the Constitution.

The National Security Agency (NSA) program for domestic spying on American citizens is a good example of how the courts' aggressive use of the standing requirement continues to frustrate attempts to pierce the veil of government secrecy. In 2005 the *New York Times* (relying on the type of unauthorized leak we discussed in chapter 4) disclosed that President Bush had authorized the NSA as part of a national security investigation to intercept telephone calls and emails of American citizens on U.S. soil without obtaining a warrant. Most legal observers felt that Bush had clearly crossed the line into illegal conduct in this instance, not only because a good case could be made that such intercepts violate both the Fourth and First Amendments but also because they appeared to be clearly in violation of the procedures that Congress had set out in 1978 in the Foreign Intelligence Surveillance Act (FISA)[26] to handle domestic national security electronic surveillance. FISA requires that the government obtain a warrant from a special federal court before engaging in electronic surveillance on American soil. So here we had a situation much like *Youngstown* and *Hamdan*; the president had not acted with congressional support, or in the face of congressional silence, but had ignored limitations that FISA placed on just this type of activity.

Although a lawsuit challenging the program was successful at the federal district court level, the Sixth Circuit Court of Appeals dismissed it in 2007 in a 2-1 decision.[27] The two judges who ruled for the government never reached the issue of whether the president had violated the Constitution or FISA because they believed that none of the plaintiffs in the lawsuit (lawyers and journalists who believed that their conversations and emails had been targeted for interception) had standing under Article III. The plaintiffs alleged that they were injured in their professional careers because potential clients and sources would not communicate with them because of fear that the government was eavesdropping on their communications. The government countered by noting that the plaintiffs had no proof that they were the targets of government intercepts and therefore they had no standing to sue. In the usual case, this factual question would be resolved by discovery procedures, but here the government claimed that the "state secrets" doctrine discussed in chapter 4 prevented such an inquiry and that the proper procedure was for the court to dismiss the case on the grounds that the plaintiffs had not shown standing. The majority agreed and dismissed the case.

This reasoning enables the government to intentionally break the law without any of its victims being able to secure a judicial declaration of the illegality of their conduct. But that odd result did not upset Judge Batchelder, the author of the lead opinion, who pointed out that a plaintiff could

> still assert his views in the political forum or at the polls. Slow, cumbersome, and unresponsive though the traditional electoral process may be thought at times, our system provides for changing members of the political branches when dissatisfied citizens convince a sufficient number of their fellow electors that elected representatives are delinquent in performing duties committed to them.[28]

If Judge Batchelder meant to suggest that the victims could work to elect new members of Congress who would pass laws prohibiting the challenged conduct, that path would appear to be inadequate since Congress had already passed such a law (FISA) that the president had ignored. He could also ignore a new law safe in the knowledge that the standing doctrine would protect him from judicial action. Perhaps the judge meant that plaintiffs had other "political" recourses; they could convince Congress (over a presidential veto) to cut off funds for the NSA program or impeach the president. But these costly and improbable political avenues do not provide a viable substitute for citizens who are only asking the federal courts to enforce the law as their official oaths require them to do.

Unfortunately, the Sixth Circuit is not alone in its belief that federal courts are powerless to remedy unconstitutional and/or illegal presidential conduct shielded by a claim for secrecy. In another case challenging the legality of the NSA program, the Ninth Circuit came to a similar conclusion.[29] In that case, the result was even more bizarre because the court knew that the plaintiffs had indeed been the target of NSA intercepts. The plaintiffs and the court knew this because the government had inadvertently given a document referring to the surveillance to plaintiffs during discovery on a related case. But the court held that the state-secrets privilege still applied and therefore they had to rule that there was no standing even though everyone knew the plaintiffs had in fact been victims of surveillance.[30]

We need to replace the current official Constitution on the issue of standing with one that permits courts to articulate the legal norms that the government must obey in the area of national security. When we look at the textual source of judicial power in Article III (reprinted in the appendix to this book), we find no limitation on the Court's jurisdiction in cases involving foreign affairs; quite to the contrary, many of the types of cases explicitly assigned to the Court's jurisdiction involve foreign affairs, such as cases between American citizens and "foreign States, Citizens, and Subjects" as well as those "involving Ambassadors, other public Ministers and Consuls. . . ." Nor does Article III make any mention of the current Supreme Court's litany of requirements to show standing: injury, causation, and redressability. The term "standing" itself does not appear in the text; instead, it limits Supreme Court jurisdiction by the more capacious terms "cases" or "controversies."

Harvard law professor Richard Fallon sets out three constitutional policies behind the Article III "case" or "controversy" requirement. First, it is geared to help courts make informed decisions by ensuring that the issues are clearly presented to judges; second, it is intended to ensure that the judicial branch does not interfere with the rights of another branch by second-guessing policy decisions; and third, it reflects a respect for judicial identity limiting the courts to disputes brought in a traditional judicial form.[31] The current Supreme Court's interpretation of the standing requirement is a grossly inefficient means of achieving any of these goals. Whether or not a plaintiff has suffered an injury has at best a very loose connection to his or her ability to set out the issues clearly for the Court to decide. In the NSA cases, there was never any doubt that plaintiffs and their counsel would do an excellent job of informing the Court about the issues—a much better job than could be done by a plaintiff who suffered technical injury but had few legal resources to prosecute the case. The NSA cases also did not involve second-guessing the executive branch on the wisdom of spying on citizens, but rather posed the question whether FISA and the First and Fourth Amendments forbade the government from engaging in such conduct, irrespective of whether it was a wise policy choice. And no one doubted that the plaintiffs' claims were presented in a traditional judicial form; the plaintiffs sought a judicial ruling on the legality of government conduct.

Any discussion of standing should begin with *Marbury v. Madison*, the case that established the Supreme Court's power of judicial review. *Marbury* is based on the premise that the Constitution as the fundamental law of the land must take precedence over conflicting legislation and that when a conflict arises it is the Court's duty to resolve it by determining the Constitution's meaning. As Chief Justice John Marshall put it, in the quotation that begins this chapter, "It is emphatically the province and the duty of the judicial department to say what the law is. Those who apply the law to particular cases, must of necessity, expound and interpret that rule."[32] We need an interpretation of the "case" or "controversy" requirement of Article III that does not prevent the Supreme Court from performing that duty.

Abraham Chayes has pointed out that Marshall's statement can be reconciled with two different models of judging. One, which Chayes calls the "private law model," emphasizes the judicial role in resolving the particular dispute, seeing the Court's primary role as that of resolving the dispute, with articulation of the constitutional norm being only a necessary side effect of its dispute-resolution function.[33] But Chayes points out that *Marbury* also supports what he calls a "public law model" that emphasizes the Court's larger constitutional role of expounding "what the law is" for the guidance of citizens and other branches of government.

Courts must perform both public law and private law functions. We need courts to settle private disputes, but this does not detract from the larger society's need to have an authoritative interpretation of the meanings of the laws. The truth of this proposition is illustrated by the Supreme Court's long-standing practice of refusing to hear the vast majority of cases appealed to it, choosing to decide only those cases that raise issues that are important to the concerns of the legal system as a whole. Yet the current official standing doctrine prevents courts from hearing many such important cases. The current standing doctrine not only detracts from the courts' performance of their full constitutional role of expounding the meaning of the Constitution and laws but also permits the executive branch, in cases like those involving the NSA spy program, to act as the effective judge of the legality of its own conduct, a violation of a basic premise of the rule of law. At a minimum this leads to unnecessary uncertainty about what the law really is. And, at worst, it condones government law breaking.

Of course a court should not accept every case filed no matter how remote the plaintiff's connection to the case or how weak his or her ability to litigate it well. The "case" or "controversy" requirement of Article III should require that the plaintiff establish some "stake" in the issue he or she wishes to litigate.[34] But the presumption should be that if the government has broken the law, some plaintiff has standing to bring the violation before the courts. All citizens of a democracy have a stake in ensuring that the government obeys the law.

In individual rights cases, this goal can be achieved by merely expanding the concept of injury. In the NSA case, the dissenting judge did this by finding that the requirement of injury was satisfied when the plaintiff showed a "reasonable fear" of being a target of illegal surveillance.[35] The Supreme Court has often accepted more attenuated forms of injury as constituting sufficient standing to permit important cases to be heard.[36]

An Active Court

Constitutional law is in the end a product of both the document's text and the Supreme Court justices who interpret it. A democracy that respects human rights and insists on separation of power requires an active Supreme Court. Yet "judicial activism" is usually used as a pejorative term in American politics in the belief that it is undemocratic. Since the Warren era, conservatives have vociferously complained about the Supreme Court's lack of a democratic pedigree.[37] What they mean is that in a democracy we should prefer that decisions be made by presidents and legislators, who are elected, rather than by judges, who are not. I think that the criticism of the Supreme Court as antidemocratic misses the mark. Once we recognize that modern democracy is more than the rule of the current electoral majority, we can see that the Supreme Court is not less democratic than Congress or the presidency; it is democratic in a different way. Supreme Court justices are nominated by elected presidents and confirmed by elected senators. The democratic control is indirect, but still effective over time. On individual rights issues like freedom of speech, this indirect democratic control leaves justices better situated than elected officials to respect constitutional values. The fact that justices do not have to face election every two, four, or six years makes them better able to consider issues on their constitutional merits than elected officials who are more likely to be unduly influenced by short-term political interests And while judges are more insulated from short-term political pressures than elected officials, the Court itself is made politically responsive in the long term by means of the appointment power. Presidents appoint justices who share their political vision, a fact that ensures that over time Supreme Court decisions tend to reflect the values of the national political majority.

It is tempting to dismiss the conservative attacks on judicial activism as being premised not so much on democracy as on disagreement with the Warren Court's human rights agenda. But in recent years scholars who support these same human rights have also attacked judicial review.[38] I am especially intrigued by Harvard Law School professor Mark Tushnet's arguments against judicial review since his larger constitutional vision is close to my own. Tushnet describes his "populist constitution" as "oriented to realizing the principles of the Declaration of Independence and the Constitution's Preamble." As the afterword to this book will make clear, I too see "the Declaration of Independence as the central document of the American political tradition."[39] But while I see an activist Supreme Court as a necessary tool towards this goal, Tushnet sees it as an obstacle.

Tushnet frames the issue of judicial review as one of institutional capacity, a matter of which branch—the legislature or the judiciary—is better situated to infuse constitutional values into their deliberations. I presume that he believes that the same arguments that favor legislators over judges also favor presidents over judges. He rejects the stereotypes that legislators only think of short-term political benefits and that judges are immune from considering the political implications of their decisions. Nor does the possession of a law degree necessarily make judges better guardians of individual rights; as we have seen, many judges have little interest in protecting individual rights. We must also concede that on some individual rights issues like a right to a good education, it is only the legislature that has the capacity to appropriate the funds necessary to make the abstract right a concrete reality. And Tushnet is correct to point out that legislators might well take their constitutional responsibilities more seriously on issues like freedom of speech if they knew that there was no judiciary to perform that task. It is difficult to drum up populist enthusiasm for issues that never come to a legislative vote, and if issues like free speech were handled by the legislature, they might receive more attention in political campaigns.

On issues of presidential power, Tushnet argues that judicial review is unnecessary because the relevant constitutional norms are "self-enforcing." He believes that Congress will protect its role in the constitutional structure against executive branch encroachment without court involvement. I think that the history of congressional action since 9/11 does not support Tushnet on this point. As the foregoing chapters have documented, Congress has for the most part abdicated its role as an equal partner in the national security arena.

Tushnet's position on the First Amendment is more nuanced. He concedes that judges may be more protective on some First Amendment issues that I have emphasized involving criticism of government conduct, but he believes that this comparative advantage for the judiciary is canceled out by the Congress's advantages on other First Amendment issues.[40] But his concession on this point supports the need for an activist judiciary, at least in the crucial area of political dissent. In fact, the populist politics he hopes for requires judicial protection of dissent, a fact illustrated by the story of the civil rights movement, told in chapter 3.

I think Tushnet is correct in cautioning us not to romanticize judges as philosopher/statespeople above political calculation. He is also correct in reminding us that an activist judiciary is not a substitute for a popular involvement in politics. But I think he fails to see how an active judiciary can complement such a politics. And judges do have institutional advantages in handling constitutional issues. Their life tenure insulates them from the short-term political calculations necessary for reelection. This does not ensure that they will look to long-term consequences of their actions, but it makes it more likely that they will do so. And Supreme Court justices are part of a long tradition of debate on constitutional values that honors independent thinking and keeps issues alive across time by means of dissenting opinions. Certainly, if we look to the recent history of the Court on national security issues after 9/11, the current conservative Supreme Court's record, while spotty, appears vastly superior to that of the Congress, even when Congress was controlled by the Democratic Party.[41] Just think what the Supreme Court's record might have been if a majority of the justices believed they had an important role to play in making sure that the government respected constitutional values. Courts also have one other important comparative advantage over legislatures: they are the one forum in which an individual, no matter how weak politically, can file a lawsuit and demand that the government respond to his or her claims.

Appointing Justices

I mentioned above that it is difficult to arouse populist interest in issues that do not come to a legislative vote. This means that it is difficult to involve voters in the way individual cases are decided, but it does not mean that we cannot better involve citizens in the way Supreme Court justices are appointed. Justices are appointed by a political process, but in truth it is not a very good one. As former Harvard Law School dean Elena Kagan points out, Senate confirmation hearings have evolved into "a vapid and hollow charade, in which repetition of platitudes has replaced discussion of viewpoints and personal anecdotes have supplanted legal analysis."[42] We need to choose justices in a manner worthy of the power and dignity of their office. Some of the problem begins with the constitutional text itself. Article II simply states that the president "shall nominate, and by and with the Advice and Consent of the Senate, shall appoint Ambassadors, other public Ministers and Consuls, *Judges of the Supreme Court*, and all other Officers of the United States" (emphasis supplied). A nominee to the Supreme Court who may serve thirty or forty years is chosen by the same process that chooses an ambassador to a small South American nation who only serves a year or two. The fact that the authors of the Constitution did not foresee the powerful role the Supreme Court was to play in our politics probably explains this anomaly.

Most modern democratic constitutions have copied the American model in providing for judicial review of constitutional issues, but they have not given judges life tenure as our system does. Instead, they usually provide for single terms of a generous but not open-ended duration. This would probably be an improvement on our Constitution because it would give justices terms long enough to insulate them from political pressures but encourage more democratic turnover on the Court. But since our Constitution is a very difficult one to amend, such an amendment is very unlikely to take place.

If a constitutional amendment is impractical, we can still improve the current process by opening it up to the same type of democratic debate we have argued for on national security issues. First, the Senate should take its "advice and consent" responsibility seriously. It should make clear that the burden is on the judicial nominee to demonstrate that he or she is qualified to serve as a Supreme Court justice. And demonstrating an acceptable political vision should be one of those necessary qualifications. The Supreme Court should be a forum of higher politics, and a nominee's larger political vision is a relevant consideration. The Senate should insist on nominees who have an ample public record to discuss and who are willing to defend that record. The nomination and eventual rejection of Judge Robert Bork in 1987 might be a useful model. Bork, a highly respected conservative scholar, was nominated by President Reagan to replace the moderate conservative Lewis Powell, who had been the deciding vote in many of the constitutional controversies of the seventies and eighties. Bork had a well-established "track record" that he defended eloquently at the hearings, but at the end of the day critics were able to show that there was good reason to believe that, if confirmed, he would not be a firm supporter of privacy and civil rights protections. Citizens' groups interested in those issues lobbied individual senators to reject Bork, and eventually the Senate rejected his nomination by a 48-42 vote. While some of the charges against Bork in retrospect seem hyperbolic, there is little reason to doubt that the Senate was correct in its determination that he was outside the political mainstream on many important constitutional issues.

Some might fear that a nomination process resembling the Bork nomination might lead to rejection of a brilliant iconoclast and the selection of more politically moderate but intellectually mediocre justices. But once we accept the fact that a Supreme Court justice's job inevitably has a political component, brilliance no longer becomes the only criterion. We do not necessarily always choose the brightest candidate for office. And history also shows that the quality of a justice's performance on the Court is hard to predict. Felix Frankfurter and William Douglas were the two great minds appointed by Franklin Delano Roosevelt, but history shows that the back-country lawyer Hugo Black proved to be at least as capable a justice as either of them.

It is inevitable that the president and the Senate will sometimes disagree on a nominee's qualifications. Such political disagreements in our system are usually resolved by a compromise, and there is no reason why this should not be the case with judicial appointments. The text says the nominee must get fifty senators to consent to his nomination, but this requirement of a bare majority can be expanded by the use of the filibuster by dissenting senators. It takes sixty votes to foil a filibuster. While there are good reasons why senators should not filibuster on ordinary legislation, the confirmation of a justice who an individual senators feel is unqualified and who will probably serve well beyond the term of the president who appoints him or her is no ordinary issue. A de facto requirement that a nominee receive the support of sixty senators would result in the appointment of justices who are perceived as being within the mainstream in their political values. This type of moderation is a reasonable demand for an office that grants great political power with life tenure. And sometimes perceived "moderates" can surprise us, as the legacies of Justices Warren, Brennan, Blackmun, Stevens, and Souter attest.

Of course, more political input into the appointment process does bring some danger that the Supreme Court would become a covert court of lower politics instead of an overt court of higher politics, as I advocate. But as the case of *Bush v. Gore*[43] attests, that nightmare scenario can play out whether or not we face up to the fact that justices wield political power. And using the filibuster to require a de facto super-majority for appointing justices would actually decrease the chances of narrow party partisans being appointed.

Since the Warren era, Republican presidents have made all but three of the appointments, and often they have chosen nominees with very conservative views who have been confirmed without strong Democratic opposition. My quarrel is not with the presidents who make such appointments; they are trying to put in place officials who will advance their agendas. One can properly blame the Democratic members of the Senate for not better performing their gate-keeping function. But if we look at the issue from a larger political perspective, the real problem is that constitutional politics has not become the important campaign issue in presidential or Senate campaigns that it deserves to be. If the Supreme Court wields the power that this book suggests, voters must become better informed on the issues justices confront so as to be able to evaluate nominees. I would like to think that books like this one can make a meaningful contribution to that process. The wide-ranging democratic debate this book celebrates must be extended to Supreme Court nominations. When the people speak, the president and the senators will listen.

Afterword

A Human Rights Constitution

The men who won our independence believed that the final end of the State was to make men free to develop their faculties; and that in its government the deliberative forces should prevail over the arbitrary. They valued liberty both as an end and as a means. —Justice Louis Brandeis

Justice Brandeis's opinion in *Whitney v. California*[1] is a classic statement of the American theory of democracy. I wish to especially focus on his insistence that we must value "liberty as an end *and* as a means" (emphasis supplied). Brandeis is speaking about the "liberty" of freedom of speech, but his point applies to a much larger set of human rights ranging from personal rights like privacy to social rights like education. Privacy and education are good things in themselves because they "make men free to develop their faculties," but they are also the means by which democracy ensures that the "deliberative forces prevail over the arbitrary."

Unfortunately, the deliberative forces do not prevail over the arbitrary today with regard to national security decisions. The president dominates the process both by word and by deed. A president's unparalleled access to the media, his ability to control the information most relevant to the debate, his symbolic status as national father figure, and his ability without the consent of Congress to commit American troops and prestige to military action undermine the democratic process that operates on other issues. To reset the democratic balance, we need both a limitation on the president's power and an expansion of First Amendment rights. We have to prohibit the president from acting before there is an informed debate that gives opposition speakers a realistic chance to have their voices heard. Here is where we need a new official First Amendment, one that grants the public access to the information necessary for an informed debate, and both protects activist groups from government harassment and provides them with full use of the public streets and parks for demonstrations that make their case.

I have argued to this point that a new interpretation of both the First Amendment and of presidential power under Article II is necessary. But if a reader were to ask whether the reforms I have advocated are sufficient to support full citizen participation in debates on national security issues that democracy requires, my answer would have to be no. While these reforms would be an important improvement over the status quo, a more ambitious vision of the Constitution is necessary if we mean to take democracy seriously. I would like to use this short afterword to sketch what this vision—one I call the Human Rights Constitution—would include.

The Human Rights Constitution furthers the project of self-government in two mutually reinforcing ways. First, it argues that each citizen should have an opportunity to participate in the national decision-making process both as speaker and as voter. But also it sees the self-fulfillment of each citizen ("to make men free to develop their faculties") as the government's primary goal. Other interests, like providing for national security, are necessary to accomplish this citizen-centered goal but can never preempt it. Government exists for the benefit of its people, not the other way around. And the goal of the constitutional enterprise is not just citizens who can participate in the governing process but individuals empowered to become the authors of their own lives. The following is a survey of the wide variety of political, personal, civil, and social rights that such a constitution should include. I hope the reader will understand that I can only suggest an agenda of issues in the space allotted.[2]

1. Political Rights

In our discussion of national security, I stressed the political dimension of the First Amendment rights of free speech, free press, and political association, but other political rights are also necessary. The conventional approach to the thorny issue of campaign finance reform asks whether legislation that limits campaign spending violates the First Amendment. I would not only give that question a negative answer but also contend that a First Amendment geared to supporting the rights of all citizens to be heard would require campaign finance reform. It's antithetical to the goal of the First Amendment to permit wealthy individuals and groups to have grossly disproportionate input into public debate.

I also talked about the importance of protecting the right of political association for free speech activists, but minority political parties also need constitutional protection. Often the hope of electoral victory makes the major political parties reluctant to embrace new ideas, but smaller, more ideologically driven parties have no such reluctance to adopt and publicize these new ideas. These small parties can play an important mediating role between free speech activists and the larger political process only if they are protected against legislation supported by the major parties designed to discourage their growth.

Finally, it is not enough that all citizens are allowed to vote; their votes must have equal weight. Voting will never represent the will of the true majority so long as the major parties are permitted to gerrymander electoral districts for their partisan advantage.

2. Personal Rights

Many human rights do not directly involve politics. Some constitutional rights are geared to protect individuals in the personal sphere, but these personal rights also have a political function. Consider the political impact of the First Amendment's Free Exercise Clause. While we do not protect the individual's personal right to believe what he or she wishes because of that right's political impact, the fact remains that churches, especially small, controversial sects, are important incubators of new ideas and must be protected against the prejudices of the majority. And history shows that often it is religious believers who are the first to stand up against government power.

Just as the Free Exercise Clause protects the individual's right to believe, the Free Speech Clause protects the privacy rights of adults to decide for themselves what to read and to view. While time, place, and manner restrictions that protect unwilling adults and all minors against offensive material are permissible, only mature adults can be the ultimate judges of what ideas they consume. This not only protects the privacy of individuals; it also protects the unconventional ideas that often are targeted by laws against obscenity and indecency.

Beyond the privacy elements in the traditional rights of free speech, political association, and free exercise of religion, a Human Rights Constitution must also explicitly recognize a more general privacy right. This right would permit the individual citizen to make certain basic decisions for himself or herself. The citizen, not the government, must decide whom to sleep with, whom to marry, when to procreate, and how to die. And while (as we discussed in chapter 5) free speech activists should have a First Amendment right of association claim to freedom from government surveillance, all citizens should be able to claim a more general privacy right that guarantees them an informational privacy right against governmental (and corporate) monitoring of their private activities.

3. Civil Rights

The United States has made significant progress in the area of civil rights by banning unjustified discrimination on the basis of race and sex. These civil rights protections not only allow individuals freedom to "develop their faculties" as they please, but they also have enabled racial minorities and women to play a larger role in our economic and political life. But these antidiscrimination rights must be extended to other groups subject to prejudice. One example might be gays seeking equal access to the institution of marriage; another would be ex-felons attempting to restart their lives. And the existence of a formal right of nondiscrimination on the basis of race can never shield defendants against necessary steps to remedy the present effects of prior state and private discrimination.

4. Social Rights

But political, personal, and civil rights are not enough. A modern democracy must also support social rights like health care and a good education. Traditional constitutional rights take the form of immunities against governmental action, but in a modern democracy we also need affirmative social rights that give citizens a claim on state resources. Every American child should have a right to a first-class education that will enable him or her both to successfully participate in the global economy and to play his or her role in American democracy. All citizens should have access to basic health care as a constitutional right.

Individual constitutional rights are traditionally enforced by the courts. We have to recognize that courts cannot do the entire job with regard to social rights because it is only legislatures who can appropriate the funds necessary for good schools or health care. This does not make social rights any less important to creating a democracy in which all citizens can fully participate, but it does require cooperation among the executive, legislative, and judicial branches of government. Courts cannot appropriate funds; but they can articulate principles and strike down legislation inconsistent with those constitutional principles.

5. Rights against Corporations

Individual constitutional rights were invented at a time when governments were the only loci of power large enough to threaten individual liberty. Now we know that corporations can be just as formidable a threat to civil liberties as public power. It does not really matter for free speech purposes whether you are fired after speaking out on a public issue by IBM or by a municipal government. Corporations are created by law and are granted many benefits by federal, state, and local governments. It is eminently fair that the Constitution should require them to respect civil liberties like freedom of speech.

I do not know whether my Human Rights Constitution will become the official interpretation of the United States Constitution. To me it is not a radical document. It only insists that all citizens have their voices heard and their votes weighted equally as well as enjoy the benefits of a good education, health care, and a zone of personal privacy. I would argue that the Human Rights Constitution is only a contemporary version of what Lincoln called "government of the people, by the people, and for the people." I think it provides an inspiring challenge to our current official Constitution. But I recognize that the victory of the Human Rights Constitution, if it comes at all, will come sometime in the future. Whether and when it comes will depend in large part on the presidents we elect and the Supreme Court justices they appoint. In that regard, the election of Barack Obama is a good sign. While we will have to wait to see what the future brings, I, like the free speech activists this book celebrates, believe that the future belongs to those who work to create it. It is in that spirit that I offer this book.

Appendix

Selected Provisions of

the U.S. Constitution

ARTICLE I:

SECTION 8. The Congress shall have the power: . . .

To define and punish Piracies and Felonies committed on the high Seas, and Offences against the Law of Nations;

To declare War, grant Letters of Marque, and Reprisal, and make Rules concerning Captures on Land and Water;

To raise and support Armies, but no Appropriation of Money to that Use shall be for a longer Term than two Years;

To provide and maintain a Navy;

To make Rules for the Government and Regulation of the land and naval forces;

To provide for calling forth the Militia to execute the Laws of the Union, suppress insurrections and repel invasions; . . .

To make all Laws which shall be necessary and proper for carrying into Execution the foregoing Powers, and all other Powers vested by this Constitution in the Government of the United States, or any Department or Officer hereof.

ARTICLE II:

SECTION 2. The President shall be Commander in Chief of the Army and Navy of the United States, and of the Militia of the several States, when called into actual Service of the United States; . . .

He shall have Power, by and with the Advice and Consent of the Senate, to make Treaties, provided two thirds of the Senators present concur; and he shall nominate, and by and with the Advice and Consent of the Senate, shall appoint Ambassadors, other public Ministers and Consuls, Judges of the supreme Court, and all other Officers of the United States. . . .

SECTION 3. He shall from time to time give to the Congress Information of the State of the Union, and recommend to their Consideration such Measures as he shall judge necessary and expedient; . . . he shall receive Ambassadors and other Public Ministers; he shall take Care the laws be faithfully executed. . . .

Article III:

SECTION 2. The judicial Power shall extend to all Cases, in Law and Equity, arising under this Constitution, the Laws of the United States, and Treaties made, . . . under their Authority;—to all Cases affecting Ambassadors, other public Ministers and Consuls;—to all Cases of admiralty and maritime Jurisdiction;—to Controversies to which the United States shall be a party;—to Controversies between two or more States;—between a State and Citizens of another State;—between Citizens of different States;—between Citizens of the same State claiming Lands under Grants of different States, and between a State, or Citizens thereof, and foreign States, Citizens or Subjects.

Notes

INTRODUCTION

1. The public outcry that arose after the Supreme Court's decision in *Bush v. Gore* (531 U.S. 98 2000) is a good example. Of course, the justices who ruled in Bush's favor denied that they were influenced by party loyalty, but after reading their opinions, constitutional law experts found that claim hard to believe. The more important point is that if the disputed election had been decided in the House of Representatives, no one would have complained about a Republican congressperson voting in favor of the Republican candidate for president.

2. *Hamdan v. Rumsfeld*, 548 U.S. 557 (2006).

CHAPTER 1

1. There are exceptions, but they tend to prove the rule. The first ten amendments, which comprise the Bill of Rights, were enacted using the Article V process, but this was a prearranged deal entered into to assure that the Constitution itself would be ratified. So too the civil rights amendments—the Thirteenth, Fourteenth, and Fifteenth—also followed the Article V procedure, but they were only able to pass because most white southern voters were not allowed to participate in the elections for the legislators who approved them.

2. *NLRB v. Jones and Laughlin Steel Corp.*, 301 U.S. 1 (1937).

3. John Yoo, *Powers of War and Peace*, 12.

4. Jack Goldsmith, *Terror Presidency*, 82-83.

5. Ibid., 198.

6. 343 U.S. 579 (1952).

7. Dean Harold Koh of Yale Law School has described Jackson's concurrence as cogently articulating "a flexible theory of decision-making premised upon separated institutions sharing powers." Harold Koh, *National Security Constitution*, 108.

8. Ibid., 106.

9. 50 U.S.C. Sec. 403(d)(5).

10. Tim Weiner, *Legacy of Ashes*, 76, 77. Weiner summarizes President Eisenhower's commitment to use of the CIA for covert activities, including "paramilitary warfare missions." He also refers to a 1963 FBI report that the CIA (with Robert Kennedy's knowledge) tried to assassinate Castro (372-73). There is no direct evidence linking John Kennedy to the plot but also little reason to believe that his brother would consent to such a plan without his knowledge.

11. Ibid., 74.

12. Arthur M. Schlesinger, *Imperial Presidency*, 158.

13. Tim Weiner, *Legacy of Ashes*, 160.

14. Ibid., 180.

15. Ibid., 372-73.

16. Ibid., 207.

17. Taylor Branch, *Parting the Waters*, 909.

18. Tim Weiner, *Legacy of Ashes*, 251.

19. See Stanley Karnow, *Vietnam*, 380-92.

20. Tim Weiner, *Legacy of Ashes*, 252-53, 301.

21. See Geoffrey Stone, *Perilous Times*, 483-88.

22. See Arthur Schlesinger, *Imperial Presidency*, 187.

23. Ibid., 187.

24. See Arthur Schlesinger, *Imperial Presidency*, 255-66.

25. Quoted in Harold Koh, *National Security Constitution*, 149.

26. U.S.C. Ch. 36.

27. 5 U.S.C. Sec. 552 et seq.

28. Tim Weiner, *Legacy of Ashes*, 357.

29. Ibid., 408.

30. Quoted in Charlie Savage, *Takeover*, 55.

31. Ibid., 56.

32. Jack Goldsmith, *Terror Presidency*, 36-37.

33. Ibid., 36-37.

34. Ibid., 36.

35. James Bamford, *Pretext for War*, 261.

36. Quoted in Charlie Savage, *Takeover*, 122.

37. Ibid., 131.

38. *Goldwater v. Carter*, 444 U. S. 996 (1979).

39. 18 U.S.C.A. Sec. 2340(1).

40. See Memorandum from Jay S. Bybee, Assistant Attorney General, to White House Counsel Alberto Gonzales, Standards of Conduct for Interrogation under 18 U.S.C. Sections 2340-2340A, reprinted in Greenberg and Dratel (eds.), *Torture Papers*, 172, 207.

41. See Charlie Savage, *Takeover*, 225.

42. See John Yoo, *Powers of War and* Peace.

43. See Jack Goldsmith, *Terror Presidency*, 87-88.

44. See Yoo, *Powers of War and Peace*, 18-19.

45. Ibid., 145.

46. See Jack Goldsmith, *Terror Presidency*, 178-85.

47. Arthur Schlesinger, *Imperial Presidency*, 2.

48. Richard Posner, *Not a Suicide Pact*.

49. See *Hamdi v. Rumsfeld*, 542 U.S. 507 (2004).

50. *Hamdan v. Rumsfeld*, 548 U.S. 557 (2006). The Court also rejected legislation proposed by the president and passed by Congress that dramatically limited the right of habeas corpus. *Boumediene v. Bush*, 128 S. Ct. 2229.

CHAPTER 2

1. See John Denvir, *Democracy's Constitution,* chapter 4.

2. Alexander Hamilton, James Madison, and John Jay, *The Federalist Papers No. 1* (Hamilton).

3. See generally, Jeffrey Tulis, *The Rhetorical Presidency.*

4. Article I, Section 7, clause 2.

5. Jeffrey Tulis, *The Rhetorical Presidency,* 135.

6. Ibid., 159.

7. H. W. Brands, *Woodrow Wilson,* 80.

8. George Creel, *How We Advertised America,* 5.

9. James Mack and Cedric Larson, *Words That Won the War,* 104.

10. Ibid., 63-64.

11. Walter Lippman, *Public Opinion,* 248.

12. Stanley Karnow, *Vietnam,* 597.

13. Reeves, *Alone in the White House,* 144.

14. Karnow, *Vietnam,* 61.

15. Ron Suskind, *The One Percent Doctrine,* 296.

16. James Bamford, *Pretext for War,* 286 (quoting Richard Clarke).

17. Bob Woodward, *Plan of Attack,* 92.

18. Ibid., 95.

19. Ibid., 119-20.

20. Ibid., 132.

21. Ibid., 120.

22. Ron Suskind, *One Percent Doctrine,* 168.

23. Bob Woodward, *Plan of Attack,* 164.

24. Ibid., 172.

25. James Bamford, *Pretext for War,* 323.

26. Ibid., 324.

27. Ibid., 324.

28. Joseph Cirincione et al., *WMD in Iraq,* 71.

29. Ibid., 70.

30. Ibid., 71.

31. James Bamford, *Pretext for War,* 377.

32. 376 U.S. 254, 271-72 (1964) (quoting *NAACP v. Button,* 371 U.S. 415 (1963)).

33. *Cohen v. California,* 403 U.S. 15 (1971).

34. Mark Hertsgaard, *On Bended Knee,* 72.

35. Bob Woodward, *Plan of Attack,* 193.

36. James Bamford, *Pretext for War,* 317.

37. See *Board of Education v. Pico,* 457 U.S. 853 (1982).

38. Thomas I. Emerson, *The System of Free Expression,* 712.

39. Steven Shiffrin, "Government Speech," 27 *UCLA L. Rev.* 565 (1980), 595.

40. Mark Yudoff, *When Government Speaks,* xv.

41. Ibid., 157.

42. *Whitney v. California,* 274 U.S. 357, 377 (1928).

43. Ron Suskind, *One Percent Doctrine,* 243.

44. Ibid., 243-48.

45. Karnow, *Vietnam,* 592.

46. Ron Suskind, *One Percent Doctrine,* 196-97.

47. Ibid., 197.

48. Such a statute was upheld in *Pestrak v. Ohio Elections Comm.,* 926 F.2d 573 (1991), but a similar statute was struck down as a violation of freedom of speech in *Rickert v. Public Disclosure Comm'n,* 168 P.3d 826 (2007).

49. See *Garrison v. Louisiana,* 379 U.S. 64 (1964).

50. *New York Times v. Sullivan,* 376 U.S. 254 (1964).

51. 376 U.S. 254, 279-80 (1964).

52. *Milkovich v. Lorain Journal Co.,* 497 U.S. 1 (1990).

53. *Austin v. Michigan Chamber of Commerce,* 494 U.S. 652 (1990); *McConnell v. FEC,* 540 U.S. 93 (2003).

54. Stephen Breyer, "Our Democratic Constitution," 77 *N.Y.U. L. Rev.* 245, 253 (2002).

CHAPTER 3

1. The First Amendment in its entirety reads as follows: "Congress shall make no law respecting an establishment of religion, or prohibiting the free exercise thereof; or abridging the freedom of speech, or of the press; or the right of the people peaceably to assemble, and to petition the government for a redress of grievances." I will use the term "First Amendment" in this book to refer to the rights of free speech, free press, and political association.

2. 205 U.S. 454 (1907).

3. 250 U.S. 616 (1919).

4. See Geoffrey Stone, *Perilous Times,* 161.

5. See Robert Cover, "The Left, the Right, and the First Amendment," 40 *Maryland Law Review* 349 (1981).

6. 250 U.S. 616, 630.

7. 274 U.S. 357, 375 (Brandeis, J., concurring).

8. 274 U.S. at 375.

9. 283 U.S. 697 (1931).

10. 299 U.S. 353 (1937).

11. 307 U.S. 496 (1939).

12. For a good overview of this period, see Geoffrey Stone, *Perilous Times,* ch. 5.

13. 341 U.S. 494 (1951).

14. See Geoffrey Stone, *Perilous Times,* 340-41.

15. I have relied on the followings works in my historical narrative of the civil rights era: Taylor Branch, *Parting the Waters;* David J. Garrow, *Bearing the Cross;* David Halberstam, *The Children;* John Lewis, *Walking the Wind.*

16. 347 U.S. 483 (1954).

17. *Abrams v. New York,* 250 U.S. 616, 630 (1919) (Holmes, J., dissenting).

18. For a good overview of "massive resistance," see Norman Bartley, *Massive Resistance.*

19. Norman Bartley, *Massive Resistance,* 193.

20. Norman Bartley, *Massive Resistance*, 210.

21. Morton Horwitz, *The Warren Court and the Pursuit of Justice*, 13.

22. See Lucas. A. Powe Jr., *The Warren Court and American Politics*, 117.

23. See e.g., *Sherbert v. Verner*, 374 U.S. 398 (1963).

24. See e.g., *Engel v. Vitale*, 370 U.S. 421 (1962).

25. See e.g., *Roth v. U.S.*, 354 U.S. 476 (1957).

26. 395 U.S. 444 (1969).

27. 395 U.S. at 446.

28. 395 U.S. at 447.

29. It should also be noted, however, that on another issue the *Brandenburg* formula was a retreat from the Holmes-Brandeis formulation. In *Whitney,* Brandeis had insisted that there must be a reasonable fear of a "serious evil" before First Amendment protection terminated. The *Brandenburg* rule allowed prosecution of advocacy of any imminent illegal action if it were likely to be acted upon.

30. 357 U.S. 449 (1958).

31. 357 U.S. at 270.

32. 372 U.S. 229 (1963).

33. 372 U.S. at 235.

34. 383 U.S. 131 (1966).

35. See *Chaplinsky v. New Hampshire*, 315 U.S. 568, 572 (1942).

36. 364 U.S. 479 (1960).

37. 376 U.S.at 270.

38. *Associated Press v. Walker*, 388 U.S. 130 (1967).

39. 380 U.S. 479 (1965).

40. 364 U.S. 479 (1960).

41. 364 U.S. at 488.

42. I have relied on the following works in the historical narrative of the Vietnam War era: Stanley Karnow, *Vietnam*; Todd Gitlin, *The Sixties*; David Maraniss, *They Walked into Sunlight*; William M. Hammond, *Reporting Vietnam*; Larry Berman, *No Peace, No Honor*; James Davis, *Assault on the Left*; Richard Reeves, *Alone in the White House.*

43. 385 U.S. 116 (1966).

44. 393 U.S. 233 (1968).

45. 394 U.S. 705 (1969).

46. 394 U.S. at 706.

47. 397 U.S. 564 (1970).

48. 393 U.S. 503 (1969).

49. 418 U.S. 405 (1974).

50. 403 U.S. 518 (1972).

51. But the Warren Court did not always protect antiwar dissent. One major refusal was *U.S. v. O'Brien*, 391 U.S. 367 (1968). In *O'Brien*, a protester who publicly burned his draft card was prosecuted under a new congressional statute that made "knowing destruction" of a draft card a felony. Congress's clear purpose was to express its outrage at the new protest tactic of draft-card burning. Instead of declaring this a form of censorship out of harmony with its earlier free speech decisions, the Supreme Court upheld the decision. .

52. 403 U.S. 15 (1971).

53. 403 U.S. 713 (1971).

54. William Hammond, *Reporting Vietnam*, 126.

55. Stanley Karnow, *Vietnam*, 561.

56. Ibid., 26.

57. See *Gertz v. Welch*, 418 U.S. 323 (1974); *Time Inc. v. Firestone*, 423 U.S. 448 (1976).

58. See e.g., *Broadrick v. Oklahoma*, 413 U.S. 601 (1973).

59. In fact, Justice Breyer wrote an excellent little book in which he argues that "participatory self-government" is one of the cardinal values in our constitutional tradition. See Stephen Breyer, *Active Liberty*.

CHAPTER 4

1. 283 U.S. 697, 716 (1931).

2. Alasdair Roberts, *Blacked Out*, 49.

3. Ibid., 45.

4. 403 U.S. 713 (1971).

5. 403 U.S. at 75,57-58.

6. 403 U. S. at 717.

7. 403 U.S. at 726-27.

8. Floyd Abrams, *Speaking Freely*, 52.

9. *Richmond Newspapers, Inc. v. Virginia*, 444 U.S. 555, 587-88 (1980) (Justice Brennan, concurring in judgment). See also William J. Brennan, "Address," 32 *Rutgers L. Rev.* 173 (1979).

10. 438 U.S. 1 (1978).

11. 438 U.S. at 32.

12. 438 U.S. at 32.

13. 5 U.S.C. Sec. 551-52.

14. 331 F.3d 918 (D.C. Cir. 2003); cert. den. 124 S.Ct. 1041 (2004).

15. 215 F. Supp. 2d 94 (D.D.C. 2002).

16. 331 F.3d at 928.

17. 331 F.3d at 940.

18. 345 U.S. 1 (1953).

19. Ibid. at 7-8.

20. Ibid. at 8.

21. Sissela Bok , *Lying: Moral Choice in Public and Private Life* (1978), 7 (quoted in Louis Fisher, *In the Name of National Security*, 22).

22. *Al-Haramain Islamic Foundation v. Bush*, 507 F.3d 1190 (9ᵗʰ Cir. 2007).

23. Senator Ted Kennedy and Senator Arlen Specter have introduced legislation— the State Secrets Protection Act—that prescribes this type of procedure.

24. Louis Fisher, *In the Name of National Security*, 165-69.

25. 418 U.S. 683 (1974).

26. 418 U.S.683, 706 (1974).

27. 408 U.S. 665 (1972).

28. Quoted in Daniel Ellsberg, *Secrets*, 432.

29. One exception to this general practice was the prosecution of Vice-President Cheney's chief aide, Scooter Libby, relating to his authorized "leak" of the fact that Valerie Plame was a CIA agent. Libby was eventually convicted of lying to the FBI. But this exception in a way proves the rule. The Plame affair caused so much political controversy that Attorney General John Ashcroft was forced to appoint a special counsel to decide whether to prosecute. Such an appointment is a rare event; in most cases of authorized leaks, the attorney general simply decides not to prosecute. Even in this case the official who made an authorized leak was given preferential treatment. President Bush commuted Libby's sentence.

30. 50 U.S.C. Sec. 421.

31. See *United States v. Morison*, 604 F.Supp. 655; appeal dismissed, 774 F. 2d 1156 (4th Cir. 1985).

32. 408 U.S. 665, 725 (1972).

33. William Hammond, *Reporting Vietnam*, 39-41.

34. Quoted in Philip Knightly, *The First Casualty*, 419.

35. Tom Gjelten, National Public Radio reporter, quoted in Robert Jensen, "Embedded Reporters' Viewpoint Misses the Main Point," University of Texas, Aug. 20, 2009, http://uts.cc.utexas.edu/~rjensen/freelance/attack61.htm.

36. See Bennett, Lawrence, and Livingston, *When the Press Fails*, 43.

37. Cass Sunstein, *Republic.com. 2.0.*

CHAPTER 5

1. *Whitney v. California*, 274 U.S. 357, 375 (Brandeis, J., concurring).

2. *United for Peace and Justice v. City of New York*, 243 F. Supp. 2d 19 (S.D. NY 2003); aff'd 323 F.3d 175 (2d Cir. 2003).

3. 243 F. Supp. 2d 19, 23.

4. 323 F. 3d 135 (2d Cir. 2003).

5. 243 F. Supp. 2d 19, 25.

6. 323 F. 3d 175, 176.

7. 243 F. Supp 2d 19, 31.

8. 243 F. Supp 2d 19, 33, fn. 15.

9. 243 F. Supp. 19, 23.

10. Christopher Dunn, Arthur Eisenberg, Donna Lieberman, Alan Silver, and Alex Vitale, *Arresting Protest: A Special Report of the New York Civil Liberties Union on New York City's Protest Policies at the February 15,2003 Antiwar Demonstration in New York City (April 2003)*,14.

11. Ibid., 19.

12. See *Coalition to Protest the Democratic National Convention v. City of Boston*, 327 F. Supp. 2d 61 (Mass. 2004); aff'd *Black Tea Socy. v. City of Boston*, 378 F.3d 8 (1st Cir. 2004).

13. 327 F. Supp. 2d at 67.

14. Id. at 76.

15. Id at 78. During the 2004 campaign, anti-Bush protesters also found that they were not allowed to attend Bush rallies to even silently express their opposition to his war policies. The rallies' sponsor, the Republican National Committee, was able

to successfully argue that under another Rehnquist Court First Amendment decision (*Hurley v. Irish-American Gay, Lesbian, and Bisexual Group of Boston,* 515 U.S. 557 (1995)), permitting anti-Bush protesters to attend a rally would unconstitutionally interfere with the rally's sponsors' right to control the message of their speech. The *Hurley* case involved an attempt by gays of Irish descent to march in the Boston St Patrick's Day parade. The Supreme Court held that to require the parade's organizers to allow the gays to march in the parade under a gay rights banner would violate the parade organizers' free speech right to control their own message. The result was to allow the Bush campaign team to create media events for television audiences that showed no sign of public opposition to Bush's policies.

16. They would not appear to explain why over one hundred thousand people came to New York City in February of 2003 to protest President Bush's plans to invade Iraq.

17. See *Menotti v. City of Seattle,* 409 F. 3d 1113 (9th Cir. 2005).

18. For a good anecdotal account of the demonstrations, see Janet Thomas, *The Battle in Seattle.*

19. *Menotti v. City of Seattle,* 409 F.3d 1113 (9th Cir. 2005).

20. 409 F.3d 1113, 1158, 1162 (Paex, concurring and dissenting).

21. *Perry Ed. Assn. v. Perry Local Educators' Assn.,* 460 U.S. 37, 45-46.

22. 491 U.S. 781 (1989).

23. 491 U.S. at 798-99.

24. 452 U.S. 640 (1981).

25. 452 U.S. 640, 654-55.

26. 534 U.S. 316 (2002).

27. 534 U.S. at 324.

28. 534 U.S. at 318 fn.1

29. *U.S. v. U.S. District Court,* 407 U.S. 297, 314 (1972).

30. Geoffrey Stone's book has an informative chapter on this time. *Perilous Times,* ch.6.

31. See generally, Geoffrey Stone, *Perilous Times,* 483-88.

32. See generally, Donner, *Protectors of Privilege,* 91 et seq.

33. *Intelligence Activities and the Rights of Americans, Book II, Part III, Subpart D, Final Report of the Senate Select Committee to Study Governmental Operations with Respect to Intelligence Operations,* United States Senate, 94th Cong. 2d Sess. 71 (4/26/76) (hereafter Church Committee Report, Book II), 211.

34. Church Committee Report, Book II, 89.

35. Cole and Dempsey, *Terrorism and the Constitution,* 93.

36. 18 U.S.C. 2709.

37. 50 U.S.C. 1801 et seq.

38. Pallitto and Weaver, *Presidential Secrecy,* 175.

39. Ibid., 189.

40. Mark Schlossberg, "The State of Surveillance: Government Monitoring of Political Activity in Northern and Central California," ACLU of Northern California, available at http://aclunc.org/issues/government_surveillance_the_state_of_surveillance_shtml. Last accessed Aug. 20, 2009.

41. See e.g., Jane Mayer, *The Dark Side.*

42. 357 U.S. 449 (1958).
43. 364 U.S. 479 (1960).
44. 408 U.S. 1 (1972).

CHAPTER 6

1. *Marbury v. Madison,* 1 Cranch 137, 177 (1803).
2. An aide in the Bush administration told reporter Ron Suskind how this system operates to the disadvantage of what he disparagingly calls the "reality-based community":

> The aide said that guys like me were "in what we call the reality-based community," which he defined as people who "believe that solutions emerge from your judicious study of discernible reality." . . . "That's not the way the world really works anymore," he continued. "We're an empire now, and when we act, we create our own reality. And while you're studying that reality—judiciously, as you will—we'll act again creating other new realities, which you can study too, and that's how things will sort out. We're history's actors . . . and you, all of you, will be left to just study what we do."

Ron Suskind, "Faith, Certainty, and the Presidency of George Bush," *New York Times Magazine,* Oct. 17, 2004.
3. 2 *Debates in the Several State Conventions on the Adoption of the Federal Constitution* (J. Elliot ed., 1866) (quoted in John Hart Ely, "Suppose Congress Wanted a War Powers Resolution That Worked," 88 *Columbia L. Rev.* 1379, 1379 (1988)).
4. 343 U.S. 579 (1952).
5. 343 U.S. at 587.
6. 343 U.S. at 637.
7. 343 U.S. at 610-11.
8. 453 U.S. 654 (1981).
9. 453 U.S. at 685.
10. Harold Koh, *The National Security Constitution,* 134-49.
11. See *INS v. Chadha,* 462 U.S 919 (1983).
12. The Jackson concurrence has also fostered a constitutional jurisprudence that fails to give sufficient guidance for future cases. The Court never addresses the extent of the president's independent power; instead it asks whether or not the Congress has approved the power by the passage of legislation at some time in the past. The key issue is always how the Court's majority will interpret the "intent" of some broadly phrased congressional statute often passed long ago. Usually the only thing that study of the legislative history of such statutes makes clear is that members of Congress had never thought about the particular power now claimed by the president. The Court determines for itself the intent of legislation long after its passage. This does result in a holding in the individual case, but since the ruling on intent is limited to a single statute and a single claimed power, it gives little guidance for future cases. So when another case arises with a new claim of presidential autonomous power, the Court must return once more to studying the intent of Congress with regard to that power.
13. 542 U.S. 507 (2004).

14. 542 U.S. at 516-17.

15. Id. at 518.

16. But while the *Hamdi* court ruled for the president on the issue of whether he had power to set up the program, it ruled against him in holding that even a congressionally authorized program must conform to constitutional limits like the Due Process Clause, and that due process required that a detainee like Hamdi be given an opportunity to challenge whether he had been properly classified as an enemy combatant. In a strange turn of events, the Bush administration, which had claimed for over two years that Hamdi was a danger to national security, suddenly changed course and sent him to Saudi Arabia, where he was set free.

17. 548 U.S. 557 (2006).

18. 548 U.S. at 593 fn. 23.

19. Id. at 594.

20. Hamdan was later convicted by a military commission of providing material support for terrorism and sentenced to five and one-half years, most of which he had already served. Pentagon officials claimed that Hamdan could still be held indefinitely after the completion of his sentence.

21. See Max Farrand, 2 *Records of the Federal Convention of 1787* (rev. ed. 1937) 318-19 (quoted in Stephen Dycus et al., *National Security Law*, 22.).

22. E.g. *Flast v. Cohen*, 392 U.S. 83 (1968).

23. 418 U.S. 166 (1974).

24. 418 U.S. at 176.

25. E.g. *Lujan v. Defenders of Wildlife*, 504 U.S. 555 (1992); *Raines v. Byrd*, 521 U.S. 811 (1997).

26. 50 U.S.C. Ch. 36.

27. *NSA v. ACLU*, 493 F.3d 644 (6th Cir. 2007); cert. den. 178 S.Ct. 1334 (2008).

28. 493 F.3d at 676 (quoting *U.S. v. Richards*, 418 U.S. 166, 179 (1974).

29. *Al-Haramain Islamic Foundation, Inc. v. Bush*, 507 F.3d 1190 (9th Cir. 2007).

30. The NSA spying program is not the only instance of illegal governmental conduct being shielded by courts' deference to government secrecy claims. Consider the case of Khaled el-Masri, a German car salesman whom the CIA mistakenly took to be an al-Qaeda leader. The agency shipped him to a secret prison where he claimed to have been tortured before they realized their mistake and released him. When he brought suit challenging this conduct, the Fourth Circuit Court of Appeals dismissed it on the ground that it was blocked by the state-secrets privilege. Even though the privilege is usually used to prevent the discovery of specific information, the court ruled that it prevents the court from hearing the case at all if the continuance of the suit will risk exposure of military secrets. *El-Masri v. United States*, 479 U.S. 296 (4th Cir. 2007); cert. den. 128 373 (2007). It is not only Mr. el-Masri who is injured by this judicial abdication, but the democratic decision-making process itself. The public loses the information these lawsuits would provide about government illegality. As citizens we all suffer a symbolic but still very grievous injury in the sense of the personal shame we feel in knowing not only that our agents engage in brutality but also that our legal system is incapable of holding them responsible for their actions.

31. Richard Fallon, "Of Justiciability, Remedies, and Public Law Litigation: Notes on the Jurisprudence of *Lyons*," 59 *N.Y.U. L. Rev.* 13-15 (1984).

32. 1 Cranch 137, 177 (1803).

33. Abraham Chayes, "The Role of the Judge in Public Law Litigation," 89 *Harv. L. Rev.* 1281 (1976).

34. *Sierra Club v. Morton,* 405 U.S. 727, 731 (1972).

35. 493 F.3d 644, 693 (Judge Gilman, dissenting) (4ᵗʰ Cir. 2007).

36. E.g. *Baker v. Carr,* 369 U.S. 186 (1962) (equal protection–reapportionment); *Regents of the University of California v. Bakke,* 438 U.S. 265 (1978) (equal protection–affirmative action).

37. Alexander Bickel, *The Least Dangerous Branch,* 16.

38. See e.g., Mark Tushnet, *Taking the Constitution Away;* Larry Kramer, *The People Themselves.*

39. John Denvir, *Democracy's Constitution,* 2.

40. Mark Tushnet, *Taking the Constitution Away,* 160-61.

41. There are not only the *Hamdi* and *Hamdan* cases discussed in the text but also the case of *Boumediene v. Bush,* 128 S. Ct. 2229 (1908), in which the Court ruled congressional legislation avidly supported by the Bush administration as in violation of detainees' constitutional right to habeas corpus.

42. Christopher Eisgruber, *The Next Justice,* 4.

43. 531 U.S. 98 (2000).

AFTERWORD

1. 274 U.S. 357, (1927).

2. I treat some of the issues at more length in my earlier book *Democracy's Constitution* (2001).

Bibliography

Abrams, Floyd. *Speaking Freely: Trials of the First Amendment.* New York: Viking Penguin, 2005.

Bamford, James. *A Pretext for War: 9/11, Iraq, and the Abuse of America's Intelligence Agencies.* New York: Anchor Books, 2005.

Bartley, Norman. *The Rise of Massive Resistance: Race and Politics in the South during the 1950s.* Baton Rouge: Louisiana State University Press 1969, 1997.

Bennett, W. Lance, Regina G. Lawrence, and Steven Livingston. *When the Press Fails: Political Power and the Media from Iraq to Katrina.* Chicago: University of Chicago Press, 2007.

Berman, Larry. *No Peace, No Honor.* New York: Free Press, 2001.

Bickel, Alexander. *The Least Dangerous Branch: The Supreme Court and the Bar of Politics.* Indianapolis: Bobbs- Merrill, 1962.

Branch, Taylor. *Parting the Waters: America in the King Years, 1954-63.* New York: Simon and Schuster, 1988.

Brands, H. W. *Woodrow Wilson.* New York: Henry Holt, 2003.

Breyer, Stephen G. *Active Liberty: Interpreting Our Democratic Constitution.* New York: Knopf, 2005.

Circincione, Joseph, et al. *WMD in Iraq: Evidence and Implications.* New York: Carnegie Endowment for Peace, 2004 (available online at www.ceip.org/files/Publications/IraqReport3.asp).

Cole, David, and James X. Dempsey. *Terrorism and the Constitution.* New York: New Press, 2006.

Creel, George, *How We Advertised America: the First Telling of the Amazing Story of the Committee on Public Information that carried the Gospel of Americanism to Every Corner of the Gobe,* New York: Harper & Brothers 1920.

Dallek, Robert. *Flawed Giant: Lyndon Johnson and His Times.* New York: Oxford University Press, 1998.

Danner, Mark. *Torture and Truth: America, Abu Ghraib, and the War on Terror.* New York: New York Review of Books, 2004.

Davis, James. *Assault on the Left: The FBI and the Antiwar Movement.* Westport, CT: Praeger, 1997.

Denvir, John. *Democracy's Constitution: Claiming the Privileges of American Citizenship.* Champaign-Urbana: University of Illinois Press, 2001.

Donner, Frank. *Protectors of Privilege: Red Squads and Police Repression in Urban America.* Berkeley: University of California Press, 1990.

Dycus, Stephen, Arthur Berney, William Banks, and Peter Raven-Hansen. *National Security Law.* 3rd ed. NewYork: Aspen, 2002.

Eisgruber, Christopher. *The Next Justice: Repairing the Supreme Court Appointments Process.* Princeton, NJ: Princeton University Press, 2007.

Ellsberg, Daniel, Secrets: A Memoir of Vietnam and the Pentagon Papers, New York: Penguin, 2002.

Ely, John Hart. *Democracy and Distrust: A Theory of Judicial Review.* Cambridge, MA: Harvard University Press, 1980.

———. *War and Responsibility.* Princeton, NJ: Princeton University Press, 1993.

Emerson, Thomas. *The System of Free Expression.* New York: Random House, 1970.

Etzioni, Amitai. *How Patriotic Is the Patriot Act? Freedom versus Security in the Age of Terrorism.* New York: Routledge, 2004.

Final Report of the Senate Select Committee to Study Government Operations with Respect to Intelligence Operations, Book II (Church Committee Report, 94th Cong., 2d Sess. 71 (April 26, 1976)).

Fisher, Louis. *In the Name of National Security: Unchecked Presidential Power.* Lawrence: University Press of Kansas, 2006.

Garrow, David J. *Bearing the Cross: Martin Luther King and the Southern Christian. Leadership Council.* New York: William Morrow, 1986.

Gitlin, Todd. *The Sixties: Days of Hope, Nights of Rage.* New York: Bantam Press, revised trade edition 1993.

Glennon, Michael C. *Constitutional Diplomacy.* Princeton, NJ: Princeton University Press, 1990.

Goldsmith, Jack. *The Terror Presidency: Law and Judgment inside the Bush Administration.* New York: Norton, 2007.

Greenberg, Karen J., and Joshua L. Dratel, eds. *The Torture Papers: The Road to Abu Ghraib.* New York: Cambridge University Press, 2005.

Halberstam, David. *The Children.* New York: Fawcett, 1998.

Hamilton, Alexander, James Madison, and John Jay, *The Federalist Papers.* New York: Bantam Dell, 1982.

Hammond, William M. *Reporting Vietnam: Media and Military at War.* Lawrence: University Press of Kansas, 1998.

Hersh, Seymour. *The Price of Power: Kissinger in the Nixon White House.* New York: Simon and Schuster, 1983.

———. *Chain of Command: The Road from 9/11 to Abu Ghraib.* New York: HarperCollins, 2004, 2005.

Hertsgaard, Mark. *On Bended Knee: The Press and the Reagan Presidency.* New York: Farrar, Straus, and Giroux, 1988.

Honigsberg, Peter. *Our Nation Unhinged: The Human Consequences of the War on Terrorism.* Berkeley: University of California Press, 2009.

Horwitz, Morton. *The Warren Court and the Pursuit of Justice: A Critical Issue.* New York: Hill and Wang, 1998.

Kalven, Harry. *The Negro and the First Amendment.* Chicago: University of Chicago Press, 1966.

Karnow, Stanley. *Vietnam: A History.* New York: Viking, 1983.

Knightley, Phillip. *The First Casualty: The War Correspondent as Hero and Myth-Maker from the Crimea to Kosovo.* Baltimore, MD: John Hopkins University Press, 2002.

Koh, Harold. *The National Security Constitution: Sharing Power after the Iran-Contra Affair.* Princeton, NJ: Princeton University Press, 1990.

Kramer, Larry D. *The People Themselves: Popular Constitutionalism and Judicial Review.* New York: Oxford University Press, 2004.

Lewis, John. *Walking with the Wind: A Memoir of the Movement.* New York: Harcourt, Brace, 1998.

Lippman, Walter. *Public Opinion.* New York: Macmillan, 1922.

Lukas, J. Anthony. *The Barnyard Epithet and Other Obscenities.* New York: Harper and Row, 1970.

MacArthur, John. *Second Front: Censorship and Propaganda in the Gulf War.* New York: Hill &Wang, 1992.

Mack, James R., and Cedric Larson. *Words That Won the War: The Story of the Committee on Public Information, 1917-1919.* New York: Russell & Russell, 1968.

Maraniss, David. *They Walked into Sunlight: War and Peace, America and Vietnam, 1967.* New York: Simon and Schuster, 2003.

Mayer, Jane. *The Dark Side: The Inside Story of How the War on Terror Turned into a War on American Ideals.* New York: Doubleday, 2008.

McWhorter, Diane. *Carry Me Home: Birmingham, Alabama: The Climactic Battle of the Civil Rights Revolution.* New York: Simon and Schuster, 200l.

Morris, Aldon D. *The Origins of the Civil Rights Movement: Black Communities Organizing for Change.* New York: Free Press, 1984.

Packer, George. *The Assassins' Gate: America in Iraq.* New York: Farrar, Straus, and Giroux, 2005.

Pallitto, Robert M., and William G. Weaver, *Presidential Secrecy and the Law.* Baltimore, MD: John Hopkins University Press, 2007.

Posner, Richard. *Not a Suicide Pact: The Constitution in a Time of National Emergency.* New York: Oxford University Press, 2006.

Powe, Lucas A. *The Warren Court and American Politics.* Cambridge, MA: Harvard University Press, 2001.

Prados, John, and Margaret Pratt Porter, eds. *Inside the Pentagon Papers.* Lawrence: University Press of Kansas, 2004.

Rabban, David. *Free Speech in the Forgotten Years.* New York: Cambridge University Press, 1997.

Rakove, Jack N. *Original Meanings: Politics and Ideas in the Making of the Constitution.* New York: Knopf, 1997.

Reeves, Richard. *President Nixon: Alone in the White House.* New York: Simon and Schuster, 2001.

Roberts, Alasdair. *Blacked Out: Government Secrecy in the Information Age.* New York: Cambridge University Press, 2006.

Savage, Charlie. *Takeover: The Return of the Imperial Presidency and the Subversion of American Democracy.* New York: Little, Brown, 2007.

Schlesinger, Arthur M. *The Imperial Presidency.* Boston: Houghton Mifflin, 1973.

Schlosberg, Mark. *The State of Surveillance: Government Monitoring of Political Activity in Northern and Central California*. San Francisco: ACLU, July 2006.

Schwartz, Bernard. *Super Chief: Earl Warren and the Supreme Court; A Judicial Biography*. New York: New York University Press, 1983.

Shane, Peter M., John Podesta, and Richard C. Leone, eds. *A Little Knowledge: Privacy, Security, and Public Information after September 11*. New York: Century Foundation Press, 2004.

Stone, Geoffrey. *Perilous Times: Free Speech in Wartime*. New York: Norton, 2004.

Strum, Philippa. *Brandeis: Beyond Progressivism*. Lawrence: University Press of Kansas, 1993.

Sunstein, Cass. *Republic.com 2.0*. Princeton, NJ: Princeton University Press, 2007.

Suskind, Ron. *The One Percent Doctrine: Deep inside America's Pursuit of Its Enemies*. New York: Simon and Schuster, 2006.

Thomas, Janet. *The Battle in Seattle: The Story behind the WTO Demonstrations*. Golden, CO.: Fulcrum Press, 2000.

Tribe, Lawrence. *American Constitutional Law*, 1st ed. Mineola, NY: Foundation Press, 1978.

Tulis, Jeffrey K. *The Rhetorical Presidency*. Princeton, NJ: Princeton University Press, 1987.

Turner, Stansfield. *Secrecy and Democracy: The CIA in Transition*. Boston: Houghton Mifflin, 1985.

Tushnet, Mark. *Taking the Constitution Away from the Courts*. Princeton, NJ: Princeton University Press, 1999.

Weiner, Tim. *Legacy of Ashes: The History of the CIA*. New York: Doubleday, 2007.

Wells, Tom. *The War Within: America's Battle over Vietnam*. Berkeley: University of California Press, 1994.

White, G. Edward. *Earl Warren: A Public Life*. New York: Oxford University Press, 1982.

Woodward, Bob. *Plan of Attack*. New York: Simon and Schuster, 2004.

Woodward, Bob, and Carl Bernstein. *All the President's Men*. New York: Simon and Schuster, 1974.

Yoo, John. *The Powers of War and Peace: The Constitution and Foreign Affairs after 9/11*. Chicago: University of Chicago Press, 2005.

Yudof, Mark. *When Government Speaks: Politics, Law, and Government Expression in America*. Berkeley: University of California Press, 1983.

Index

About the Author

John Denvir is Research Professor of Constitutional Policy at the University of San Francisco School of Law. He is the author of *Democracy's Constitution: Claiming the Privileges of American Citizenship* and editor of *Legal Reelism: Movies as Legal Texts.*